D0881331

Marxism, Class Analysis and Socialist Pluralism

Marxism, Class Analysis and Socialist Pluralism

A THEORETICAL AND POLITICAL CRITIQUE OF MARXIST CONCEPTIONS OF POLITICS

Les Johnston

Rolle College, Exmouth

London
ALLEN & UNWIN
Boston   Sydney

Allen & Unwin (Publishers) Ltd,
40 Museum Street, London WC1A 1LU, UK

Allen & Unwin (Publishers) Ltd,
Park Lane, Hemel Hempstead, Herts HP2 4TE, UK

Allen & Unwin, Inc.,
8 Winchester Place, Winchester, Mass. 01890, USA

Allen & Unwin (Australia) Ltd,
8 Napier Street, North Sydney, NSW 2060, Australia

First published in 1986

British Library Cataloguing in Publication Data

Johnston, Les
  Marxism, class analysis and socialist pluralism:
  a theoretical and political critique of Marxist
  conceptions of politics.
1. Communism
I. Title
320.5'315   HX73
ISBN 0−04−301239−6
ISBN 0−04−301240−X Pbk

Set in 10 on 11 point Baskerville and
printed in Great Britain by Anchor Brendon, Tiptree, Essex

Acknowledgement

The author and publishers would like to thank Routledge & Kegan Paul for permission to use material from the author's article 'Marxism and capitalist possession', *Sociological Review*, vol. 32, no. 1, (1984), pp. 18−37, in Chapter 2 and Chapter 3 of this book.

Preface

References to works cited in the text are given by author and date, with full details of publication being provided in the Bibliography. In the case of works by Marx and Engels, the original date of each work is given, and where page references are cited these relate to the English language editions listed in the Bibliography.

Contents

1

Marxism and the materialist conception of politics

To anyone situated on the political left in Great Britain during the last decade the period has been a peculiar and frustrating one. On the one hand, there has been a huge output of socialist theoretical work in the fields of politics, cultural studies, literary criticism and the like, much of this being inspired by developments in Marxist theory. On the other hand, in the practical sphere of politics — the parties of the left and the Labour movement — there seems to be a lack of popular support and ideological cohesion. Indeed, many of the successes to which the left can lay claim in the last decade have arisen from activity outside the sphere of the traditional socialist movement — in the women's movement, CND, civil rights campaigns and so on.

Now clearly, one cannot blame this state of affairs only on the inadequacies of socialist theory, for there are many factors contributing to the problems of the left. Having said that however, it will be suggested here that at least some of those problems relate to serious deficiencies in socialist thinking. The purpose of this book is to present a sustained critique of Marxist political theory, since that has been the most influential theoretical tradition during the last two decades. Particular attention will be directed at the inadequacies of the 'materialist conception of politics', to the problems (and in some instances pseudo-problems) which it poses and to the strategic shortcomings which are related to its adoption. It is suggested that certain of the assumptions which Marxists consider basic to socialist analysis need to be subjected to serious critical attention. Once this is done we can begin to ask some of the questions which socialists have been unwilling or unable to address. Do classes, as Marxists and for that matter many non-Marxists have assumed, constitute social agents in any meaningful sense? Does the concept of 'class interest' have any coherent meaning? If not, how does one identify socialist interests? Where do such interests reside? If interests do not reside in classes, what is one to make of the conventional Marxist view that the state 'represents' class interests? Indeed, what of the view associated with that position that the state is a relatively cohesive and unitary representative of the dominant class? Is the state unitary, or does it comprise a set of disparate and sometimes conflicting apparatuses?

We address these and other questions by developing a systematic theoretical critique of the materialist conception of politics. The basic premise of this work is that that conception of politics, despite the many recent sophisticated attempts to remedy its difficulties, has constituted a positive obstacle to the development of an effective socialist political theory. Such a theory, it is suggested, will need to be based upon a pluralistic politics, rather than a materialist philosophy.

It should be said at the outset that the 'Marxism' to be discussed here is by no means homogeneous. In the 1960s there was a naive certainty about what Marxism was. The 'Althusserian Revolution', for all its dogmatism, put a stop to such naivete by drawing a distinction between the 'essence' of a text (to be revealed by a 'symptomatic' reading) and its 'appearance'. Though no less dogmatic in its assumption of an 'essential' Marxism than were those dogmatists who insisted upon a 'naive' reading of what Marx 'said' or 'did' (Clarke, 1980, p. 27), Althusserianism did, for the first time, put the question of how Marxism is theoretically constituted on the agenda.

Over the last half-dozen years that challenge has provoked a real crisis in Marxism, a concern for the discovery of an 'authentic' Marxism, giving way to some recognition of discrepancies and inconsistencies within a discourse that is heterogeneous rather than unified. This is hardly surprising. Since the 1960s Western Marxists have been confronted by a variety of alternative Marxisms; humanistic Marxism; structuralist Marxism; Leninism; Trotskyism; Gramscism; Maoism; Castroism; African Marxisms, and so on. Moreover, the emergence of important political movements — blacks, women, ecologists and the like — some with a socialist persuasion, but many of whom questioned the right of Marxists to represent their interests, sparked off further challenges to theoretical orthodoxy.

The effect of this is to produce a serious dilemma for Marxists. Is Marxism a discourse which, despite its variations, enjoys some fundamental unity? Or is it infinitely catholic, today's orthodoxy being yesterday's heresy? Those who argue the first case insist that all Marxists accept certain fundamental truths — society as 'totality', the primacy of class struggle, the priority of relations of production and so on (see McDonnell and Robins, 1980, p. 215). This may be true, but it misses the point, for the problem of Marxism is *how* such truths are to be theorized.

An author whose work is certainly closer to the second proposition is Cottrell. He recognizes not only that there are various Marxisms but that there are also inconsistencies and contradictions within the classical texts. The Marxism he proposes is defined neither in terms of its 'materialism', nor in terms of any fundamental truths. Instead, it is the product of the political or 'discursive' priority given to 'the transformation of social relations in the direction of socialism' (Cottrell, 1984, p. 2). Since this raises obvious questions — notably the matter of how this 'Marxism' is distinguished from other socialisms which advocate similar priorities — Cottrell is obliged to find another principle of unification. Perhaps predictably, we come back to a statement of what Marx 'does' in certain crucial texts.

Cottrell's recognition of the diversity and inconsistency within Marxism does, however, raise a serious problem. In the absence of a homogeneous discourse, what is a critique of Marxism to address? One solution would be to suggest that such a critique is impossible, as the differences within and between Marxisms render the very term 'Marxism' redundant. That evades the issue however. The existence of diversity does not preclude all resemblance, though such resemblance has to be carefully qualified.

What is proposed here, then, is a conceptual means whereby an object ('Marxism') can be constituted, for the purposes of discussion and critique. The conceptual apparatus called into being for this purpose, given our concern to assess Marxism as a political and strategic discourse, will be referred to as the 'materialist conception of politics'.

Before outlining the scope of the materialist conception of politics, it is important to emphasize what is *not* being said. To invoke the materialist conception of politics is to suggest that all Marxisms share certain general theoretical assumptions. It is not to suggest that these assumptions unify Marxism. Nor does it suggest that different Marxisms theorize these basic propositions in the same way. For example, though it is maintained that Marxists share materialist ontological and teleological assumptions, it is evident that different Marxisms conceive these assumptions in different ways; compare Stalin's conception of historical transition (*Dialectic and Historical Materialism*) with Gramsci's rejection of an economistic history (*The Revolution Against 'Capital'*). Moreover, nowhere is it maintained that the materialist conception of politics constitutes a methodology. In Chapter 8 it will be seen that neither Marxist discourse nor its politics are the determinate effects of a conceptual structure. To say that discourse is not an effect of its concepts is not to say, however, that concepts and assumptions do not have effects on discourse. Indeed, one of the things which is suggested here is that Marxist ontology and teleology place certain constraints on what can be 'thought' within Marxist-socialist discourse. That discourse is, therefore, not determined by its concepts, but these concepts limit the parameters of the discourse.

The materialist conception of politics

In attempting to elucidate a materialist theory of the 'specificity of the political', Hall argues that such a theory has to suggest *some* form of correspondence between classes and politics. Without this, he insists, one is led 'to forfeit the first principle of historical materialism: the principle of [the] social formation as a "complex unity", as an "ensemble of relations"' (Hall, 1977, p. 47).

This view, which provides us with an excellent starting point, is based on two philosophical assumptions. First, there is a materialist ontology. Hall is emphatic that all Marxisms conceive society as some sort of totality structured by the primacy or relative primacy of material production. Though Marx's 1859 *Preface* has been subjected to a variety of readings by 'reductionist' and 'non-reductionist' Marxisms alike, it outlines a theoretical object (the economic structure of society, the 'real foundation' on which rises a legal and political superstructure) which, however varied its theoretical interpretations, has remained a central problem for consideration.

There is, less obviously, a second philosophical assumption at work here, that of teleology. A teleological discourse is one containing some conceptual principle of hierarchical ordering whereby social forms may be regarded as a realization or expression of their position in a conceptual structure. In some cases this merely amounts to historicism. Marx's *Preface* outlines the historical processes to which ontologically defined objects are to be subjected — the conflict between forces and relations of production and its inevitable effects. Though many Marxisms, including Marx's, are neither consistently nor primarily historicist, they may be affected by teleological assumptions. For example, Marxism is limited in its conception of socialism since this has to be conceived as the teleological antithesis of capitalism.

Given these philosophical assumptions and their possible effects, what are the characteristics of the materialist conception of politics? It is suggested here that there are six broad features.

(1)   Marxism is distinguished from other political discourses by its materialist mode of analysis. Marxists insist that political knowledge can only be gained from, and political strategy based on, an understanding of the structure of definite modes of production.

(2)   According to Marxists, politics and the state are neither natural nor functional components of society. Politics, ideology and culture may be regarded as a more or less complex representation of economic class relations. For Engels, materialism involves

> tracing political conflicts back to the struggles between the existing social classes and fractions of classes created by. . .economic development and [proving] the particular political parties to be more or less adequate political expressions of these same classes and fractions of classes. (1895, p. 187)

This view assumes that classes comprise, albeit at some ultimate level, the essential agents of political practice, politics being conceived as a process of class conflict. It is the antagonistic relations between classes which conditions the social and political structure.

(3) It is not merely the existence of classes which is important, but the particular form of class relations in which they are inscribed. When Marx talks about an analysis of class revealing 'the hidden basis of the entire social structure and with it...the corresponding specific form of the state' (1864, p. 790), he is signifying the importance of an historical examination of varying forms of economic exploitation — an historical materialism. This materialist conception of politics and history attempts to produce a *general* theory which can reveal the secret of *specific* political forms, a matter on which more will be said later. Obviously, then, the presentation of history as 'class struggle' is more than a rhetorical flourish, for Marx insists that it is not the almost universal 'fact' of economic exploitation, but its particular historical 'form' which is the key to social and political analysis. The priority given to the form of extraction of surplus labour is crucial in several respects. First, an understanding of it reveals the 'corresponding specific form of the state', of law, culture and ideology. Secondly, it indicates not only the nature, but the limits and possibilities placed on forms of political intervention in any society. Finally, it reveals the protagonists of politics to be classes of exploited and exploiting agents.

(4) This final revelation has a crucial strategic significance for socialist politics. Indeed, in Engels's view, socialism was 'no longer an accidental discovery of this or that ingenious brain, but the necessary outcome of the struggle between two historically developed classes — the proletariat and the bourgeoisie' (1880, p. 410). Even in the absence of such an historicism, however, the discovery of the 'secret' of exploitation to which Engels refers is fundamental to Marxist political strategy. For it is Marx's claim that relations of production are simultaneously relations of exploitation and it is the contradictions engendered in exploitation which structure politics.

The link between classes in conflict and determinate forms of politics is provided by the concept of 'class interest', classes possessing objectively defined interests by virtue of their polarized locations in the structure of exploitation. (Though this is the basis for Marx's definition of class interest, he sometimes complements it with other aspects. In the case of working class interests, for example, he invokes the idea of the proletariat as a 'universal' class. This means either that the working class is a majority class (Marx and Engels, 1848, p. 118), or that their interests are genuinely 'social' interests (Marx, 1844, p. 333). Both of these are, however, supplementary to Marx's view of the objective source of class interests.) The class antagonisms which condition the political sphere are, therefore, grounded in the process of economic exploitation. In consequence, Marxist political analysis is invariably concerned with the problem of class analysis.

(5)   This is not to say that Marx always claims objective interests to be manifested in political practices. Indeed, Marx is ready to recognize that some form of political organization may be required to play a role in the generation of interests. Marx does insist, however, that the problem of the organizational conditions of interest formation be conceived as a problem of 'class-consciousness' — notably in his famous distinction between 'class in itself' and 'class for itself'. This subsumption of questions of political organization to class consciousness reaches extreme lengths amongst some Marxists: 'party. . .organization corresponds to a stage in the class consciousness of the proletariat' (Lukacs, 1971, p. 304), though it has been evident in less extreme forms throughout the history of Marxism (see Ollman, 1972). As we shall indicate, this is a facet of the Marxist teleology and the particular forms of subjectivism associated with it. What is important for present purposes, however, is to observe that in the materialist conception, political interests are conceived as the necessary representational attachments of classes. In Chapters 7 and 8 the reader will discover that some recent 'revisionist' Marxisms have attempted to conceive interests in non-class terms, whilst still retaining the representational form of analysis which Marxism invokes, a position which reproduces classical problems in a new form.

(6)   Finally, and perhaps most significantly, is the question of 'reductionism', for the class-based conception of politics described here might appear to sanction an economistic reading of politics which simply reduces the political to a manifestation of economic class relations.

Historically Marxism has been pre-occupied by the problem of reductionism and this issue has no more dominated debates than in the last decade. The denigration of cruder economistic versions of Marxism has been based upon refined and sophisticated attempts to present the 'base/superstructure' model of Marx's *Preface* in a non-reductionist form. Most major Marxist writers of the twentieth century, from Lenin, Gramsci and Mao to present-day structuralists and their critics, have concentrated attention on this problem. Indeed, many of the dominant concepts in Marxist political debate — 'relative autonomy', 'overdetermination', 'hegemony' — have arisen as an attempt to resolve the problem of reductionism. Consider, for example, Meszaros's attempt to establish a necessary connection between the problem of 'specificity' and the concept of 'relative autonomy':

> One cannot grasp the 'specific' without identifying the manifold inter-connections within a given system of complex mediations . . . Marx's assertions about the ontological significance of economics become meaningful only if we are able to grasp the Marxian idea of manifold

specific *mediations* in the most varied fields, which are not simply 'built upon' an economic base but also actively *structure* the latter through the immensely intricate and relatively *autonomous* structure of their own. (1972, p. 115)

Now it is by no means accidental that some of this conceptual refinement has been forged in political struggles of a decidedly 'practical' nature, for above all else, it is the purportedly erroneous *strategic* consequences of a reductionist reading of politics which has led Marxism to concentrate attention upon the theoretical elucidation of the 'specificity' of politics. Marxism has continually insisted that an effective socialist political analysis must be both materialist *and* able to identify political agents, relations and structures in a non-reductionist form.

In much of what follows a variety of 'non-reductionist' Marxisms will be evaluated in terms of their strategic utility for socialist politics. The form of criticism made here, however, will be rather different from conventional ones, since it is suggested that the strategic limitations of Marxism are not due to reductionism so much as theoretical and political incoherence. Indeed, it will be argued that the problem of reductionism that has so pre-occupied Marxists and their critics is very much a pseudo-problem.

Finally, there are one or two points which should be made clear to the reader concerning the content and 'style' of the book. First, it should be emphasized that this is a book about class *analysis*, not a book about class '*structure*', as people understand that term. What this means is that the book is not primarily concerned with the substantive question of class boundaries (e.g. the distinction between middle and working classes); nor is it concerned with the location of particular groups of agents in relation to the class structure (e.g. the unemployed, blacks, women). If the reader seeks a 'classification' of the British social structure, this is not the place to find it.

Instead, our concern is with the theoretical object class analysis. Class analysis is a political project with a set of theoretical assumptions concerning class agency, class interests, and the forms by which those interests are represented in politics. It is towards an evaluation of this political project, rather than to an empirical account of places and positions in the 'class structure', that our concern is directed. For this reason it is emphasized (see especially Chapter 6 below) that our intention is not to offer a detailed, let alone definitive, review of Marxist literature on class boundaries and class locations. This would be pointless because it is the very project of class analysis, rather than the substantive arguments of class analysts which is the object of criticism. Ultimately our concern is with the erroneous conception of political interests and objectives that the project of class analysis underpins. Inevitably this raises questions about the place of class in socialist theory; questions which are not reducible to the matter of how agents may be located in or around the class structure.

Secondly, it is appropriate to say something about the frame of reference adopted. It is suggested here that there can be no general theory of socialist politics. Such a suggestion depends upon a particular conception of social relations, aspects of which may originally be traced to Foucault, though whose main source in a socialist context can be found in *Marx's 'Capital' and Capitalism Today* by Cutler, Hindess, Hirst and Hussain. Drawing on these arguments it is suggested that social relations cannot be conceived as a totality. In the case of Marxism, society constitutes a mode of production with a determinate relationship between its elements. That relationship is posited, we suggest, on the basis of certain epistemological, ontological and teleological propositions. In the absence of these propositions and the general causal mechanisms they support, that totalistic conception of social relations becomes impossible to sustain. What we are instead confronted with is a plurality of social relations enjoying no necessary coherence or unity.

One problem which this position immediately throws up concerns the relationship between different sets of relations. In the case of the politics of 'the left', for example, how is the relationship between different discourses (socialism, feminism, ecology, gay liberation, black politics, etc.) to be articulated? ·

There can be no general answer to that question. Any response has to be related to determinate sets of social agents and their objectives. Accordingly, any such response has to be a limited one. Our appeal to socialist pluralism is, therefore, programmatic rather than prescriptive. This fact indicates a stylistic difference between the approach taken here and that adopted by some other writers. For example, we do not believe it possible to decree the relationship between discourses which are themselves far from cohesive and unitary (in contrast to some of the literature relating to the articulation of socialism and feminism). Our intention is the much more limited one of trying to indicate some of the issues which might be at stake in any future articulation. This is the purpose which lies behind much of the discussion of popular democracy in the final chapter. Here we take the view that democracy, far from being a solution to the problem of articulation, is merely an objective, the adoption of which will require socialists and others to make choices between different social constituencies, their aims and interests.

The argument which follows is divided into four sections. The first (Chapters 2 and 3) examines Marxist analysis of the capitalist enterprise and property ownership. In the second section (Chapters 4 and 5) we consider the various Marxist approaches to the problem of the capitalist state. Section Three (Chapters 6 and 7) looks at the role of class analysis in socialist political calculation. The concluding section (Chapter 8) has two purposes. First, it draws together theoretical conclusions about reductionism, corporate enterprise, the state and class analysis. Secondly, it makes some suggestions about the implications such conclusions might have for socialist politics, arguing specifically for a 'pluralistic' approach to socialism.

Marxism, Managerialism and Capitalist Possession

2

Marxism and the problem of the managers

The problem of management has pre-occupied both Marxist and non-Marxist writers for almost a century. Such a pre-occupation derives from the theoretical centrality which the managerial function holds in both types of discourse. For example, the assertion by non-Marxists that society is 'post-capitalist' rests almost entirely upon the theory of managerialism. According to this view the 'capitalist' has disappeared from the economic sphere to be replaced by the figure of the 'manager'. This suggestion rests upon the claim that Western economies have experienced a 'separation of ownership and control', the emergence of the joint-stock company (JSC) signalling a break in the traditional unity of property. Ownership becomes dispersed amongst a multiplicity of shareholders who cease to hold any effective control over the activities of the enterprise. Such control becomes the prerogative of managerial employees who lack ownership rights in the company. By virtue of this alleged separation the proponents of managerialist theory maintain that capitalist property relations are superseded. Capitalism gives way to 'post-capitalism'.

It should be clear, then, that Marxists have considered the refutation of managerialism a fundamental part of their economic analysis, for if it is to be maintained that the economy remains capitalist in form, some convincing rejoinder has to be made to the theory of 'separation'. Indeed, it is more serious than this, for managerialism provides a set of propositions which offer a challenge to Marxism's very theory of society. It is no exaggeration to say that postwar non-Marxist sociology was built upon a foundation inspired by managerialism. This is obvious if one considers some of the main themes of that sociology. First, it is maintained that the dissolution of property which arises from the separation of ownership and control has general implications for the class structure of Western societies, a rigid system of classes giving way to a more flexible system of stratification. Secondly, it is argued that the emergence of a managerial stratum breaks the traditional link between property and power which is said to underpin the capitalist state. Some versions of post-capitalist theory maintain that power now passes to those possessing specialized or technical knowledge; some that power is placed in the hands of a bureau-cratic–managerial elite; some that power becomes diffused in a pluralistic political system where economic power no longer dominates, but is used for socially responsible ends. Thirdly, it is claimed that a managerially dominated economy is one where the traditional orientation to profit maximization is absent. Managers have, it is suggested, a variety of bases from which to exercise their 'discretion' other than naked economic interest. In the same way that profit maximization as an economic ideology disappears from the economy, it may be claimed that there is a general 'end of ideology' throughout society. Social decision-making becomes less affected by considerations of political ideology and more the product of purely technical calculations.

Together these propositions constitute the basis of a fundamental critique of Marxism. Most of this chapter is devoted to examining some of the attempts which Marxists have made to rebuff the theory of managerialism. In doing this we concentrate not merely on the substantive content of this work but also on the theoretical assumptions which underpin it. One thing which this approach reveals is the surprising similarity between managerialists and their Marxist critics on certain basic points, a matter which will be pursued more fully in Chapter 3. But first we consider how managerialists conceive capitalism and private property. It is crucial to understand these conceptions in order to con-textualize both managerialism and the Marxist response to it.

Managerialism, capitalism and private property

Let us begin by considering some of the classical managerialist arguments in a little more detail. For this purpose it is useful to distinguish the two broad strands of managerialist theory which Nichols has encapsulated in the terms 'sectional' and 'non-sectional' (1969, p. 43).

The 'non-sectional' version of managerialist theory is most adequately represented in the work of Berle and Means. Here, it is argued that the typical business enterprise of the nineteenth century which was both owned and managed by individuals or small groups has been supplanted. It is replaced by great corporations 'under unified control and manage-ment' where 'hundreds of thousands of workers and property worth hundreds of millions of dollars, belonging to tens or even hundreds of thousands of individuals', are combined (Berle and Means, 1935, p. 3).

The separation of ownership and control which has supposedly arisen in these circumstances is based, then, on the emergence of the JSC, a development which, in Berle and Means's view, produces a dispersal of ownership of the means of production. The dispersal of ownership of shares which has taken place has, it is said, led to a situation where the modern corporation is 'owned' by hundreds of thousands of unconnected shareholders.

Together with this has emerged a corresponding change in the relationship of control of the means of production. The property owner has, in Berle and Means's view, changed his position of owner-manager for one where he is simply the recipient of the wages of capital. There exists, then, a body of owners who exercise virtually no control over the operation of the means of production. In fact, it is suggested that owners no longer own physical means of production, but 'pieces of paper'. Control over physical means of production is now vested in managers, the so-called 'New Princes'.

A large part of Berle and Means's work is, in effect, directed at elaborating upon the nature of control in the modern business enterprise. In the original work a number of distinct forms of control are identified; control through ownership; control through a legal device; majority, minority and management control (Berle and Means, 1935, ch. 5). Though any combination of these strategies may co-exist, their analysis of the two hundred largest US corporations suggests that managerial control is increasingly dominant, managers becoming the 'new economic autocrats'.

However, Berle and Means are far from suggesting that managerial control necessarily leads to a managerial domination contrary to social interests. Instead, they suggest that the separation of ownership and control has cleared the way for the community 'to demand that the modern corporation serve not alone the owners or the control but all society'. Indeed, in their view it is essential that if the corporate system is to survive, its control 'should develop into a purely neutral technocracy' (Berle and Means, 1935, p. 356). Berle, writing thirty years later, clearly believes that such a situation has evolved, for managers are now seen to be endowed with a 'corporate conscience' which demands that they act in a socially responsible manner, in accordance with the 'public consensus' (Berle, 1960, pp. 90–1 and 110).

Burnham's 'sectional' version of managerialist theory is both constructed on different theoretical principles and reaches quite different substantive conclusions from Berle and Means. Although Burnham's work is highly inconsistent and, in consequence, difficult to summarize succinctly, three main themes may be identified. First, it is claimed that 'the instruments of production are the seat of social domination' (Burnham, 1945, p. 89). A managerially controlled economy is, thus, also a managerially controlled society. Managerialism, in effect, replaces political ideologies such as capitalism, socialism and fascism around which social and political domination has previously been constructed. Secondly, the 'managerial revolution' is dependent upon increased state ownership of the means of production. This raises one question for Burnham. If state ownership deprives individuals of property rights, how can there be a ruling class? His answer to this is 'comparatively simple'. Managers will rule, not because they control the means of production directly, but because they have indirect control 'through their control of the state' which itself owns the means of production. In short, the state 'will, if we wish to put it that way, be the "property" of the managers' (Burnham, 1945, p. 65). Thirdly, since in Burnham's view, managers, like any other controllers of the means of production, will exercise such control in their own interests, it follows that all conceptions of a 'socially responsible management' are to be rejected.

Despite obvious differences between the two 'classical' positions it is apparent that they share very similar conceptions of capitalism and private property. Marxists, and indeed many non-Marxist writers, would accept that capitalism is a system of commodity production involving a money economy, where possession of the means of production is in private hands and a 'separated' category of wage labourers is employed to produce profit. Managerialist conceptions of a capitalist economy are, however, notable in one particular respect in that they equate 'private' ownership of the means of production with individual ownership. In Dahrendorf's view, for example, capitalism can only be said to exist when the continued 'union of private ownership and factual control of the means of production' can be demonstrated. What this amounts to is the demand that a 'typical capitalist' be identified, who is 'at the same time', legal owner of the factory, manager of production and commander of the workforce (Dahrendorf, 1959, p. 40).

Without doubt, the clearest expression of this view is found in Burnham, for whom 'capitalism' is equated with production under the domination of 'capitalists' and, therefore, for whom private enterprise is synonymous with individual enterprise. Burnham insists that the capitalist class is 'comprised of those who as individuals own . . . the instruments of production', private enterprise being based upon private property rights vested in 'individuals as individuals' (1945, pp. 18, 23 and 111). This attempt to equate capitalism as a system of economic production with an ideal type of classical entrepreneurial capitalism is adopted by other writers in the managerialist tradition, many of whom see capitalism as necessarily founded upon a '*laissez-faire*' ideology which supports individualism and the 'invisible hand' of market forces.

Clearly, any form of collective proprietorship or state control of enterprise signals the end of capitalism for writers in this tradition. Burnham argues that state intervention 'beyond a certain point' is incompatible with the continued existence of private production, since such intervention has to lead to the elimination of capitalists from the economy. In his

view, the capitalist state is of a peculiarly limited type, since an extension
of state ownership amounts to a reduction of capitalist property:

> You cannot call an economy of state ownership capitalist because in it
> there are no capitalists. A capitalist is one who, as an individual, has
> ownership interests in the instruments of production; who, as an individual,
> employs workers, pays their wages, and is entitled to the product of their
> labour. (Burnham, 1945, p. 103)

The point at stake here is not whether an economy with state-run
sectors can be called capitalist, but whether Burnham's attempt to
polarize the categories of private ownership and institutional ownership
is valid. For, in making this polarization, Burnham assumes that institutional, collective, or corporate possession are incompatible with
private possession of the means of production. It is that proposition
which is at the core of the managerialist argument and which needs to be
evaluated.

Marxism and the class position of managers

Because the theory of managerialism has provided the main support for
post-capitalist theory a great deal of the Marxist analysis of capitalist
possession has been directed to its analysis. What is most striking,
however, is that discussion has tended to concentrate not on managerial
function in the production process, but on the problem of the 'class
position of managers'. The precise reason for this, and its significance,
will become clear in what follows.

In the Marxist view, capitalism as a system of production involves
relations between two categories of agent, those who possess the means
of production and those who are separated from such possession. The
fundamental pre-condition of capitalist relations of production is, therefore, the purchase and sale of labour power. Such purchase and sale is
dependent upon the availability of labour power, which, in turn, rests
upon the presence of certain legal conditions that sanction the existence
of 'free' wage labour and private ownership of the means of production
(Marx, 1867, pp. 146–7). Though this characteristic form (purchase
and sale of labour power, involving a set of agents of possession and a set
of wage labourers) and its conditions of existence, are recognized as
fundamental to the analysis of capitalist relations of production, Marxist
analysis of management does not always grant them centrality. Although it
might appear evident that managers constitute a category of wage
labourers, separated from possession of the means of production, Marxists
frequently seek to establish 'class divisions' within managerial wage

labour, assigning certain sections to a 'new middle class' and other sections to the class of capitalist possessors. Braverman is typical of this latter strand of thought:

> We must consider the possibility of the same form [purchase and sale of labour power] being made to conceal, embody and express other relations of production . . . the fact that the operating executives of a giant corporation are employed by that corporation and in that capacity do not own its plant and bank accounts, is merely the form given to capitalist rule in modern society. These operating executives by virtue of their high managerial positions, personal investment portfolios, independent power of decisions, place in the hierarchy of the labour process, position in the community of capitalists at large etc., etc., are the rulers of industry, act 'professionally' for capital and are themselves part of the class that personifies capital and employs labour. (Braverman, 1974, pp. 404–5)

To a certain extent Braverman's statement amounts to a synopsis of the Marxist approach to management and direction. Such an approach attempts to identify the manager as 'capitalist' by precisely the sort of characteristics Braverman identifies; wealth and connections; behavioural motivations; domination of the labour process; appropriation of surplus value or of profit from the production process; performance of the function of 'non-labour'; ownership of shares. In all of this, then, Marxism accepts that the relevant agent of capitalist possession under current conditions is the manager, but that, contrary to managerialism, this agent is fundamentally capitalist. Let us consider some of the attempts to argue this position in a little more detail.

Management as a capitalist elite or stratum of capital

Managerialism is principally characterized by its claim that the motivation of the manager is less geared towards simple maximization of profit than that of the classical entrepreneur. The most simplistic Marxist response to this view of 'soulfulness' is a retort to such motivational analysis which rests, more or less, on motivational categories. Thus, it is claimed that managers do, in fact, exhibit a profit motive no less severe than that of capitalists. To this end it is frequently considered necessary to establish the 'social backgrounds' and 'connections' of managers in order to show that, as a group, they act relatively cohesively in the interests of capital, property and wealth. Indeed, much of this type of analysis converges with the sociological analysis of elites.

Typically, such an analysis would reject the view that managers act with social responsibility. For Miliband, the structural imperatives of capitalism render it inherently 'selfish' so that 'the single, most important purpose of businessmen, whether as owners or managers, must be the pursuit and achievement of the "highest possible" profits . . . that "selfishness" is inherent in the capitalist mode of production' (1969, p. 34). The manager will then, irrespective of his personal motives, be directed by 'the economic logic of the market' (Blackburn, 1972, p. 168).

Along with this, an emphasis may be placed upon the fact that managers attract high salaries (Miliband, 1969) or are employed in positions where perquisites and tax advantages predominate (Blackburn, 1967). In addition, it may be argued that managerial shareholding is itself a characteristic of modern business corporations, a fact which, it is said, calls managerialist theory into question (Miliband, 1969; Blackburn, 1972; Westergaard and Resler, 1975; Scott, 1979). All of these factors may be said to contribute to the existence of a managerial stratum which is 'the most active and influential part of the propertied class' (Baran and Sweezy, 1968, p. 46).

Perhaps the clearest exposition of this type of argument appears in Zeitlin's influential article. He insists that a coherent analysis of the modern business corporation has to be rooted in the examination of its class structure. Corporate action will therefore be investigated by concentrating on phenomena such as interlocking directorships, networks of shareholding, the characteristics of those who control banks, and so on. Such an approach employs the family as its unit of analysis, looking in particular at kinship relations between officers, directors, and principal shareholders in corporations. In short, this type of investigation is based upon exploring the relationship between 'concrete interest groups or classes' (Zeitlin, 1974).

This type of position is very much based upon the notion of '*social* class' analysis, an approach which leads to a considerable degree of convergence with the sociological analysis of elites. In both cases the project is to identify members of a stratum of the capitalist class. By arguing that the capitalist class has a membership united by intermarriage, similar educational backgrounds, comparable patterns of socialization, and frequent social interaction, two things may be maintained. First, that managers are capitalists: 'Far from being a separate class, they constitute in reality the leading echelon of the property-owning class' (Baran and Sweezy, 1968, p. 46). Secondly, that the capitalist class is united, a theme which we shall consider more fully in the next chapter:

> whatever the situation within the corporation as the predominant legal unit of ownership of large scale productive property, the 'owners' and 'managers' of the large corporations, taken as a whole, constitute different strata or segments — when they are not merely agents — of the same more or less unified social class. (Zeitlin, 1974, p. 1078)

Though the type of argument described here has provided the basis for much Marxist discussion of senior management and direction, it is clearly subject to severe difficulties if it is to be judged as a piece of Marxist theory. Some of these difficulties are obvious. First, Marxism is adamant that distributional factors, such as income, cannot define class position. Marx, himself, insists on this point:

> Vulgar common sense turns class differences into differences in the size of one's purse . . . the size of one's purse is a purely quantitative difference, by which any two individuals of the same class may be brought into conflict. (Cited in Bottomore and Rubel, 1963, p. 244)

Secondly, Marxists frequently contend that multiple or factorial definitions of class are sociological rather than Marxist. Thirdly, it is usually suggested that the analysis of motivation and social interaction is foreign to Marxism, since Marxists place priority upon structural factors in the determination of action.

The validity of these arguments need not concern us. What is more important is that they have caused Marxists to seek a more rigorously materialist definition of the manager's class position. For some writers this has involved trying to integrate class analysis in general, and the examination of management in particular, into the conceptual structure of the labour theory of value.

Managers as appropriators of surplus value or of profit

Given this objective, one approach to the problem has been to define managers, not as wage labourers *per se*, but as appropriators of surplus value or of profit, and, therefore, as capitalists. For Poulantzas this has the added advantage of pre-empting any speculative discussion of managerial motivation: 'For Marx, profit is not a motivation of conduct − even one imposed by the system − it is an objective category that designates a part of realized surplus value' (Poulantzas, 1972, p. 244). According to this view managers are, in essence, paid out of the profits of the enterprise. This position is echoed by Westergaard and Resler who regard managers as having a capacity to demand payment from profits by virtue of the fact that they 'have their hands on the till' (Westergaard and Resler, 1975, p. 162).

There is, unfortunately, little to support this argument. In the first place, none of these authors specifies the mechanisms whereby such appropriation takes place, nor how managerial payments are separated off from those of other wage labourers. But, apart from that, Marx himself explicitly argues against the view, for he claims that the 'salary of the manager is, or should be, simply the wage of a specific type of skilled labour, whose price is regulated in the labour market like that of any other labour . . . [the wages of a manager] are entirely divorced from profit' (Marx, 1864, pp. 386 and 436). Managers cannot, therefore, be designated appropriators of surplus value or of profit in any sense consistent with Marx's meaning of those terms.

At this point we might take stock of where our comments on the two positions so far discussed leave us. Our criticism up to now has been restricted to showing that both arguments have a dubious status when judged as pieces of Marxism, since their theoretical assumptions seem to clash with basic propositions of Marxist theory. But this hardly constitutes an adequate critique, particularly in the context of a work which will show that some of these propositions are themselves problematic. In order to evaluate these positions more rigorously, therefore, we need to address them in a slightly different way. In this respect, one thing which can be considered is the underlying theoretical assumption which they adopt. A second concerns the consequences of that adoption. When we consider them in this way it is possible to make two important observations.

In the first place it would seem that both positions assume the legal conditions surrounding the production process to have no significance. Each assumes, for example, that the manager's status as employee is a mere legal formality, hiding his true character as member of the capitalist class and appropriator of profit. This is precisely the point behind Braverman's claim that under contemporary capitalism the 'same form' (the purchase and sale of labour power and the legal conditions which sanction it) might 'conceal' other relations of production. But it is by no means clear where this argument leads us, whatever its immediate and superficial appeal might be. What, for example, are we to make of the legal conditions of existence of capitalist relations of production? Are we merely to assume their analysis as insignificant? If not, and they possess this peculiarly illusionary character, how are we to know their real status and effect? What we are suggesting here is that Braverman's basic assumption about the law has far greater significance and implication than it might appear to have at first sight. There is, in particular, an unstated, yet uneasy assumption, that possession and appropriation might be built upon no legal foundation whatsoever, a matter we will consider in more detail later.

Our second observation concerns what appears to be a total lack of concern with the question of economic calculation and direction by any of the authors so far discussed. This appears to follow from the attempt to reject managerialism by showing the continued existence of capital accumulation by a capitalist class. Whatever merit this position might have, the manner in which it is presented here seems to suggest any analysis of the processes governing economic decision-making to be irrelevant. This is, indeed, the basis of Westergaard and Resler's claim that managerialism should be rejected because it 'assumes that decisions are actually *made* on a matter which is not a subject for decision . . . the aim of profit is simply taken for granted'. (1975, p. 164)

Now, it may well be true that capitalist enterprises do take the aim of profit for granted, but it is no less true that that aim will be subjected to definite forms of decision by economic agents. Moreover, such decision will have definite effects on 'profitability' and the like. In other words, we have here a set of problems about economic decision-making processes within the capitalist enterprise which require serious consideration.

Management as 'non-labour'

Both of the issues referred to above arise in Carchedi's attempt to address the problem of managerial class position by using the concept 'non-labour' derived from Marx's theory of value. The analysis so produced is based upon a particular conception of the 'capitalist production process' which is said to derive from Marx. In 'Capital' Marx says of the production process that 'considered . . . as the unity of the labour process and the process of producing surplus value it is the capitalist process of production' (1867, p. 179). In Carchedi's view, then, the capitalist production process involves two distinct sets of relations of production:

(i)   Those of the labour process, involving producer and means of production in 'labour'.

(ii) Those of the surplus value producing process, involving producer, means of production and non-producer or 'non-labourer'.

It is Carchedi's view that the 'functions of capital' (those functions performed either by managers or capitalists) are non-labour. That is to say, they are functions performed 'outside the labour process but inside the capitalist production process'. The theoretical justification for this view is again derived from Marx, this time from the discussion of the 'double nature' of the labour of supervision and management (Marx, 1864, pp. 383−4). In this discussion it is claimed that any co-operative form of labour requires co-ordination and unification, a job which is productive. On the other hand, however, such labour also necessitates a role of supervision to be performed, the more it is characterized by an antithesis between producer and owner of the means of production. For Carchedi, the former category (co-ordination and unity) is an aspect of the relations of production of the labour process, nowadays carried out by a collective labourer. The latter, on the contrary, is an aspect of the relations of production of the surplus value producing process, a 'function of capital' characterized by the performance of 'non-labour'.

Carchedi uses this distinction as a means of designating certain managers 'capitalists' and others as 'new middle class'. The way in which this position is reached can best be illustrated by considering the way he distinguishes classes in a more general sense. In doing this, he draws upon Lenin's famous definition, where classes are described as

> large groups of people differing from each other by the place they occupy in a historically determined system of social production, by their relation (in most cases fixed and formulated in law) to the means of production, by their role in the social organisation of labour, and, consequently by the dimensions of social wealth of which they dispose and the mode of organising it. Classes are groups of people, one of which can appropriate the labour of another owing to the different places they occupy in a definite system of social economy. (Lenin, 1919, p. 421)

Leaving aside the question of the adequacy of this definition, what is important is that Carchedi uses the concepts of value theory to simplify it. For example, 'place in a historically determined system of social production' reduces to a distinction between producer and non-producer; 'role in the social organisation of labour' to a distinction between labour and non-labour. This type of argument enables Carchedi to define the two major classes of the capitalist mode of production (CMP) by a dichotomy. Capitalists are non-producing, exploiting, non-labouring, owners. Workers are producing, exploited, labouring, non-owners. In consequence the 'new middle class' can be defined by a combination of these factors (Carchedi, 1977, p. 5).

In the case of management, the argument may be stated as follows. In so far as the individual capitalist of private capitalism performed both labour (work of co-ordination and unity) and non-labour (work of control and surveillance) he had a dual class determination (Carchedi, 1977, p. 87). He was both proletarian and capitalist ('old middle class'), only being capitalist in the last instance because of his ownership of the means of production. In the current stage of capitalism, the functions of capital are now performed by a 'bureaucratic structure' rather than by individuals. This structure may, in itself, be divided up on a class basis, along the same dichotomous lines described above. Thus, that segment of the managerial—bureaucratic structure which performs non-labour and owns the means of production is the 'new capital personified'. That segment which performs both labour and non-labour and does not own the means of production has membership of the 'new middle class'.

Carchedi's position has been summarized at some length because of its relative sophistication when contrasted with the two positions previously described. However, his analysis appears to reproduce some of the other difficulties which were observed above. In the first place, he seems to be entirely unconcerned with the legal foundations of possession. Like most contemporary Marxists he is rightly concerned to draw a distinction between 'legal ownership' and 'real ownership' (Carchedi, 1977, pp. 13, 30, etc.). But like many other theorists he uses that distinction to justify an avoidance of any analysis of the function of law. There may well be a distinction between 'legal ownership' (as it is understood by Marxists and non-Marxists alike) and 'real ownership', though more will be said on that issue in Chapter 3. But it does not follow from this that possession is subject to *no* legal conditions, nor that such conditions do not have substantive effects.

Secondly, a real tension exists between, on the one hand, concepts of possession or ownership (relations of production, or class relations in the strict Marxist sense) and, on the other hand, the concepts of value analysis. Though that tension is inherent in Marxist analysis (a factor which we shall consider in Chapter 6) some of its effects appear very clearly in Carchedi's work. In particular, the essentialism of labour that dominates his argument tends to make any analysis of ownership redundant. Indeed, Carchedi's position is striking for its failure to address the problem of ownership in any systematic way. Where the problem is addressed it is considered in an arbitrary fashion. For example, ownership is introduced into the discussion of the 'individual capitalist' in a rather opportunistic way, to establish that figure as 'capitalist' rather than merely 'old middle class', and to avoid the embarrassment of arguing for a CMP without a capitalist class. It is, therefore, not without significance that we are told the relation connecting the three elements of the production relations (ownership/non-ownership; productive/unproductive labour; labour/non-labour;) 'cannot be discussed here' (Carchedi, 1977, p. 46). It cannot be discussed because Marxists have consistently failed to elucidate the relationship between value analysis and class analysis.

A third serious problem follows from Carchedi's essentialist position regarding labour and in particular his reduction of the social division of labour to a distinction between labour and non-labour. Despite the fact that a substantial part of the text is devoted to the analysis of the 'function of capital', one gains no insight into what managerial functionaries actually do. This is not surprising in view of Carchedi's pre-occupation with assigning them to class positions through the essentialism of labour. In the last instance his proudest boast is to claim that 'it is now possible to prove scientifically that the manager, even though he expends human activity does not work' (Carchedi, 1977, p. 112, note 56). Apart from the fact that this can hardly be regarded as the discovery Carchedi feels it to be — functionaries of capital can never work because that is precisely what defines them as functionaries of capital in the first place — it leaves the matter of direction and economic decision-making unresolved.

Moreover, it has to be said that the conception of the capitalist production process as a dualism of two sets of relations of production is untenable. It is this initial premise which relegates discussion of relations of 'ownership' to a secondary level since they become relations of production which merely intervene after production has occurred. It is clear, then, why Carchedi only introduces discussion of ownership as an afterthought. But this position is an impossible one. There cannot be a production process taking place under no determinate relationship of possession of the means of production (Cutler *et al.* 1977, p. 257). In addition to that, the view that agents of possession or their functionaries do not perform a function in the labour process is absurd. The dualistic view of the capitalist production process is untenable. There is only one labour process and both capitalists and their functionaries perform definite functions in it, functions which have important effects and which Marxists therefore need to theorize.

Marxism and managerialism: some theoretical considerations

So far, we appear to have reached something of an impasse. We have identified managerialism as the basis for a sustained critique of Marxist and socialist economics. Yet we have shown that Marxist attempts to confront it, by showing the manager to be the 'new capital personified', are without firm theoretical foundation.

This chapter will conclude with a consideration of some theoretical issues. Our intention here is to outline a number of major theoretical dilemmas which the present analysis points to. By identifying these dilemmas within Marxist theory we will, in Chapter 3, be able to tackle the question of managerialism from a different direction. For, rather than showing that Marxists have failed to resolve the problem, we shall suggest two things. First, we will establish that some of the theoretical misconceptions adopted by managerialists are, in fact, shared by Marxists. Secondly, we shall suggest that the attempt to resolve the problem of the 'class position of managers' is, in itself, problematic. It is not merely that attempts to resolve the problem are unsuccessful. The problem is entirely misconceived. For the moment, however, let us indicate some of those theoretical problems, a consideration of which will provide a basis for discussion in the following chapter.

In outlining the theory of 'separation of ownership and control' it was suggested that managerialists, whatever the particular form of managerialism they adopt, share a peculiarly individualistic conception of economic relations. This leads them to the view that capitalism is an economic system run by 'capitalists', and that 'private' property is always and only the property of individuals. According to this position, corporate capitalism, the form of economic system which would seem to be dominant in the West, would constitute an impossible economic formation. As an economic system, 'corporate capitalism' would be, to put it bluntly, a self contradiction.

One issue we need to consider, however, is the way that Marxists conceive economic agents and relations. In particular, it needs to be asked whether Marxism is able to theorize institutional and corporate forms of possession any better than managerialism. From the analysis we have presented so far there would appear to be some grounds for doubt on this matter. For example, it is apparent that many Marxists are still pre-occupied with identifying the exploiting individual — the 'Our Friend Moneybags' — of Marx's 'Capital'. This is clearly the intention behind those various attempts to define managers as an elite, or stratum of the capitalist class. In this case, the identification of agents of capitalist economic relations depends upon the existence of individuals with those subjective capacities and attributes deemed appropriate to a 'capitalist'.

The alternative approach has been to maintain that individual human subjects and their capacities are secondary in importance to structural factors. It is these structural factors, it is maintained, which shape human subjectivities. In Poulantzas's view, profit is an objective category, not a subjective motivation. Individual human agents merely 'personify' capitalist relations.

At first sight, this position might appear to avoid many of the obvious pitfalls of subjective analyses. However, we need to consider the precise significance of the concept 'personification', particularly with respect to its place in Marxist economic theory. For it is by no means apparent that the structural emphasis adopted by many Marxists avoids the problems of subjectivism. Nor is it, therefore, clear that Marxism is able to provide a coherent theory of a capitalism in which supra-individual possession is the dominant form. The following chapter will consider these matters fully.

A second difficulty concerns what we have seen to be Marxism's unwillingness to pay serious attention to the problems of decision-making within the enterprise. This shortcoming derives, to a considerable extent, from the teleological component of materialist analysis. For Marxism's main response to managerialism's teleology of 'post-capitalism' has been to assert the alternative teleology of historical materialism. What this amounts to is the claim that society, far from being 'post-capitalist', is, in fact, 'monopoly capitalist'. Indeed, in its identification of the agents of possession which are said to 'personify' capital, Marxism has a definite view of such agents fulfilling the historical mission of the materialist teleology. In consequence, the particular economic functions and roles of economic agents are of only superficial importance. Since capitalists and their functionaries are mere 'character masks', there is no real commitment to investigating the nature of the functions of direction and management. Again, some of the implications of this will be discussed in Chapter 3.

A third area of difficulty which has been discussed above is the problem of law. Marxist theory, in accordance with the materialistic premises upon which it is based, asserts the priority of capitalist relations of production over and above their conditions of existence. In the case of law we have seen that the legal conditions surrounding ownership are either ignored completely, or, at best, seen as an ideological gloss obscuring the true relations of production. In Chapter 3 we will pay particular attention to Marxism's attempt to resolve the problem of legal relations. It will be demonstrated that the failure to resolve this question leaves Marxists without a coherent theory of corporate capitalism.

3

Marxism, managerialism and corporate capitalism

In the previous chapter three areas were identified which are problematic in Marxist theory. Is Marxism able to produce a coherent theory of capitalist possession? What are the theoretical consequences of teleology for an analysis of the capitalist enterprise? Does the materialist theory of law provide an adequate basis for theorizing capitalist relations of production? Each of these themes provides a basis for the discussion which follows, though it needs to be borne in mind that there is a substantial overlap between the three problems.

Marx and capitalist production

Economic agency in Marx

In *Capital* Marx provides certain basic concepts for analysing the agent of possession under capitalist relations of production. Both these concepts and the analysis which follows from them depend, however, upon the fundamental assumption that individual agents constitute mere 'bearers' of social relations. This means that Marx's analysis deals with such agents solely 'as personifications of economic categories, embodiments of particular class relations and class interests' (1867, p. xix).

The most sustained attempt to develop that position may be found in the work of Althusser who shows that Marx's political economy begins from a total rejection of the 'homo oeconomicus' of classical economics. Instead, Marx's analysis develops from the concept of 'mode of production' and the contradictory unity of forces and relations of production that comprise it (Althusser, 1969, pp. 109–10).

The implication of this is not only that the structure of the social totality given in the mode of production determines the character of the agents which function in social relations (as 'personifications'); ultimately it is the structure of that totality, and the processes which give it its direction and momentum, that constitute the 'true' agents of social relations. For Althusser (Althusser and Balibar, 1975, p. 180), the 'true subjects' are the relations of production, the class relations which individuals merely personify. That suggestion is reasserted in Althusser's discussion of the concept 'subject' in ideology. Here, the crucial recognition concerns the ambiguity which surrounds the concept. In the case of Christian religious ideology, for example, 'subject' designates both 'subjectivity' (individuality) and 'subjection' (to a super-subject, in this case God). Hence, for Althusser, 'there are no subjects except for and by their subjection' (1971, p. 169).

Althusser produces a view of social relations similar in many respects to Marx's own. For Marx, *Capital* seeks to pierce the 'outward appearance' of capitalism and gain access to the 'inner essence'. According to this view, capitalist social relations depend upon individual action, only in so far as that action realizes the imperatives of capitalist laws of motion.

Let us consider the case of competition. In Marx's view capitalist competition exposes 'the inherent laws of capitalist production in the shape of external coercive laws having power over every individual capitalist' (1867, p. 255). Here, individual capitalists are mere elements of 'total social capital', each being 'an individualized fraction . . . of the aggregate social capital' (1863, p. 355). At the level of 'capital in general' then, the actions of individual capital units are only important for the results that they necessarily produce. Indeed, Marx maintains that the actions of units are the very means by which the 'laws of motion' are worked out on the concrete terrain. Competition is therefore merely 'inner tendency as external necessity' (1857–8, p. 414), another case of the inner-essential laws of capitalist development being effected through concrete actors. Accordingly, Marx sees the capitalist as no less circumscribed than Althusser's Christian subject. For it is capital which is set free by competition, not capitalists. The latter's actions merely appear as freedom when, in reality, they are 'the most complete subjection of individuality under social conditions which assume the form of objective powers' (Marx, 1857–8, p. 652).

Marx makes it clear, then, that the individual capitalist's participation in 'free' competition is simply the means for re-creating the conditions of capitalist production, such conditions being already present in the CMP as structured totality. The CMP thus constitutes a contradictory unity of forces and relations of production, a totality whose effects are already contained within itself (Cutler *et al.*, 1977, p. 123). At the level of social agents, these effects are realized by virtue of the fact that such agents, though 'inessential', in that they merely embody 'structural' processes, are, in fact, endowed with essential characteristics. It is because agents are essentially 'persons' that they can 'personify'. It is because they are humans that they have the subjective capacities of experience and consciousness necessary for capitalist economic relations to be effected in the personified form. As Marx himself suggests

> the laws imminent in capitalist production manifest themselves in the movements of individual masses of capital, where they assert themselves as coercive laws of competition, and are brought home *to the mind and consciousness of the individual capitalist* as the directing motives of his operation. (1867, p. 305, emphasis added)

The implication of the Marxian view of agency is, therefore, clear. Economic agents of possession ('capitalists') or their functionaries ('managers') merely obey the imperatives of the laws of motion of the CMP. On the one hand, capitalist economic relations are essentially relations between persons. On the other hand, the content of their action is given in the structure of the CMP. Before pursuing the question of this dichotomy further, however, let us investigate more fully the teleological laws of motion which economic agents are said to personify. In the context of the present discussion, this matter can best be examined by a consideration of Marx's analysis of ownership, management and the JSC.

Marx and the JSC

The same teleology which specifies the lawful constraints on the actions of economic agents also influences the treatment of ownership. Marxism has always borne an ambiguous relationship to the theory of 'separation of ownership and control', arguing that Marx was the first to theorize such a separation, but objecting strongly to the connotations which have been placed on it by non-Marxists. Where non-Marxist theorists argue that the emergence of the JSC has given rise to 'post-capitalism', contemporary Marxists claim that it is a characteristic of 'advanced', 'late', or 'monopoly' capitalism.

Marx's treatment of the JSC is inseparable from the general perspective of historical materialism and from his view of the transition process between capitalism and socialism, for it is Marx's view that such a transition is inherent in the contradictory structure of the CMP. Socialism is inevitable because capitalism contains not only the seeds of its own destruction, but also the relations of production of the emerging socialism. Socialism is the 'negation' of capitalism contained within capitalism. That is the meaning of the claim that 'capitalist production begets with the inexorability of a law of Nature, its own negation' (Marx, 1867, p. 789).

The real barrier to capitalism, then, is capitalist production itself. The more capitalist forces of production are 'socialized' the more they come into conflict with private property relations. This general process defines the inherent contradictions which shape the laws of motion of capitalism. For example, the more productiveness of labour is improved by technical means (the rising organic composition of capital and relative surplus value production), the greater is the tendency for the rate of profit to fall.

The view that capitalism contains the structural preconditions of socialism has an important influence on Marx's treatment of the JSC. For Marx, the capital upon which the emergent JSC rests implies a truly 'social mode of production' (1864, p. 436) where capital no longer takes the form of 'private capital' but is genuinely 'social capital'. The JSC is the site of those contradictions between socialized productive forces and private relations of production and appropriation which Marx regards as signifying the transition process itself. Though still a form of capitalist enterprise, it is both 'the abolition of capital as private property within the framework of capitalist production itself' (Marx, 1864, p. 436) and a 'transitional phase' in the development towards 'outright social property'.

Apart from the moralism which Marx inserts into this discourse (the JSC is regarded as synonymous with 'parasitic' finance capitalists and 'swindlers'), two main themes deserve to be commented on. Firstly, Marx's analysis points to the centralization of capital which leads, in turn, to cartels and monopoly. Monopoly is, however, merely another indication of the intensifying contradictions of capitalism, for 'the monopoly of capital becomes a fetter upon the mode of production which has sprung up and flourished along with it and under it' (Marx, 1867, p. 789).

For later Marxists, of course, the crucial question has been that of when those contradictions that constitute the so-called 'monopoly stage' will bring about the promised transition. But questions of time scale apart, all are agreed that the stage is 'transitional'. Though Lenin, for one, would admit that the monopolist—imperialist stage does not preclude the rapid growth of capitalism, he is none the less emphatic that we are witnessing capitalism in transition or 'moribund' capitalism (Lenin, 1916, p. 153). This conception of a 'monopoly stage' of capitalism has, in fact, provided the chief Marxist response to managerialism and has constituted the theoretical core of its theory of the enterprise.

Of equal significance is a second factor. Marx's view of the emergence of the JSC and monopoly as a 'mere phase of transition to a new form of production' involves a particular conception of the distinction between the 'social' and the 'private'. The JSC represents the beginnings of a new 'socialized' mode of production because in both its composition as a form of capital and in the typical form of 'co-operative' factory that develops with it ('a social concentration of the means of production and labour power'), it signifies the demise of the individual as agent of economic processes. JSCs and 'co-operative' factories represent transitional forms of capitalism because, for Marx, the socialization of the forces of production which is involved in the centralization of capital is synonymous with 'the expropriation of the means of production from all individuals' (1864, p. 439). Marx believes that because the capitalist disappears from the production process capitalism is being socialized.

Like managerialism, then, the 'separation' between ownership and management which Marx recognizes is one which leads, in his view, to the supersession of capitalism, though not in the way that managerialists have argued. For Marx, capitalist production in its transitional form involves a process where 'only the functionary remains and the capitalist disappears as superfluous from the production process' (1864, p. 388). It is that 'separation' which is the site of socialized production. The demise of the individual capitalist signifies a transition, not to the 'soulful' society of managerialists, but to a parasitic, decaying, rentier capitalism. This constitutes the very germination of socialism.

It should now be possible to draw some conclusions from the two areas considered here and relate them to the problem of management. In this respect, a number of problems in the Marxian analysis may be identified.

In the first place, Marx conflates the agent of possession under capitalist relations of production with the figure of the 'capitalist'. This is an inevitable consequence of the view that agents 'personify' class relations and embody the structural processes inherent in the structure of the CMP. In turn, this conception of agency is a necessary consequence of the theoretical structure of the materialist teleology itself. The realization of teleological processes is only made possible by the existence of individual subjects with the essential capacities of 'persons'. Accordingly, it has to follow that if no individual agents exist to 'personify' capitalist relations of possession, capitalism is being superseded (socialized).

It is because of the conflation of 'possessor' with 'individual' that Marxists have been unable to theorize corporate forms of possession. Moreover, recognition of that theoretical failing has obvious consequences, for once the equation of economic agent with individual is rejected, economic relations can no longer be conceived as effects of the structure of the CMP in the way that Marxism has argued. If economic agents are not reducible to individuals, then economic relations cannot be seen as a 'personification' of the alleged laws of motion of capitalism.

Secondly, Marx's failure to theorize capitalist possession adequately is also due to the theoretical consequences of the materialist ontology. Marx argues that the 'mode of production of material life' determines the character of the 'legal and political superstructure'. In his view 'juridical relations' reflect 'real economic relations' (1867, p. 56). The JSC is simply an effect of the socialization of the forces of production. As an institution, it is merely a reflection of the structure of the CMP, and a transitional one at that. Marx fails to consider that it is an effect of the existence of certain legal conditions; conditions which are in no way a product of developments in the productive forces; conditions which are, moreover, an outcome of political struggles between competing forces (Hunt, 1936). There is some justification in the view, then, that Marx's analysis is 'naively apolitical' (Hirst, 1979, p. 137).

Thirdly, there is the problem of the 'class position of managers'. Marxism's concentration on this problem arises as a consequence of Marx's theory of the JSC. Marx does argue for a separation of ownership and management, but the managerialist interpretation of such a separation is rejected by all Marxists. Such a rejection requires some modification of Marx's position. Whereas Marx is concerned to show the disintegration of capitalism, contemporary Marxism's main retort to managerialism is to show capitalism to be alive and kicking (if not particularly 'well').

Since these theorists share the Marxian conception of economic agency, it is necessary for them to identify a class of individuals who 'personify' capitalist relations. Managers, in short, have to be 'classified' as 'capitalists'. Because Marx offers no theoretical means for the analysis of non-individual/corporate forms of possession, it follows that the continued existence of capitalist relations can only be established if managers are defined as 'capital personified'. Marxism is not, then, concerned with the problem of what managers do. It can, after all, reassure itself that managers, like entrepreneurs, obey the external laws of the CMP and in so doing, reproduce capitalist relations. Conversely, the absence of a class of individual possessors ('capitalists', 'managers') has to signal the demise of capitalism.

Fourthly, it is clear that Marx's analysis of the JSC not only fails to provide an adequate basis for theorizing capitalist relations of production, it also seriously misconceives the political pre-conditions of socialism. The analysis is problematic in two respects. There is no incompatibility between the so-called 'socialized' productive forces of corporate capitalism and capitalist relations of production. Indeed, the corporation, far from being merely a transitional phenomenon, is the dominant form of capitalist enterprise in the current period. Moreover, the suggestion that corporate capitalism signals embryonic socialism denies the fact that socialist transformation depends upon the creation of definite political conditions which will not 'follow on' from the development of the productive forces in a certain direction.

Marxism, managerialism and the law

So far, we have considered two related problems in Marx's analysis. It has been shown that the structural theory of agency rests upon a subjective essentialism which makes the analysis of corporate action impossible.

Linked to this are the problematic effects of the materialist teleology, as outlined above. What now needs to be considered is the problem of law and in particular the question of the legal conditions necessary to sanction possession. In order to do this, we shall consider two areas. In the first of these we shall examine the managerialist theory of law and Marxism's response (or more accurately its failure to respond) to it. In the second we consider the Marxist analysis of shareholding and legal ownership.

Legal conditions and their effects

Managerialist writers, like Marx, regard 'private' property as, essentially, individual property. Berle's definition is worth quoting:

> Property is in essence a relationship between an individual (or perhaps a group of individuals) and a tangible or intangible thing . . . In law the essence of proprietorship was the owner's capacity to exclude everyone but himself from possession, use or control . . . Growth of the corporate system changed that . . . Two or three individuals 'incorporated' their business; *it was still small, still capable of being possessed.* They were stockholders, but they were also directors and managers . . . so long as the business and corporation continued small, the stockholders largely determined what the corporate title holder actually did . . . Enlargement of the corporation made it evident that fissures on the surface of property represented a clear division. (Berle, 1960, pp. 60–1, emphasis added)

The point on which this entire argument hinges is Berle's claim that 'small scale' business is the only one 'capable of being possessed', the emergence of corporate forms of enterprise leading to the destruction of 'the unity that we commonly call property' (Berle and Means, 1935, pp. 6–7). That claim depends, in turn, on an individualism which deems legally recognized corporate forms of possession to be illusory; that is to say, the law may recognize corporate possession, but in 'fact' it merely hides a 'separation' within the relation of property – a separation which calls that concept into question. For if Berle's argument is to be accepted, the concept of corporate property is an impossible one.

Burnham's conception of the law is no less dismissive. We are told, for example, that control of the instruments of production is the crux of legal right to property, the concept of 'property right' merely 'summing up' such control (Burnham, 1945, pp. 53 and 82). In this respect, it is noticeable that Burnham distinguishes legal and economic relations in a peculiarly 'economistic' fashion, 'economic facts' being demarcated from mere 'legal concepts'. One is led to assume that in Burnham's view, then, economic relations are always factual whilst legal relations may well be 'fictional'.

Though more sophisticated, Dahrendorf's argument is very similar. One of the crucial components of his thesis is a sustained critique of Marx's conception of property. According to Dahrendorf, property may be viewed in two ways; as control of the means of production, or as a legally recognized statutory property right. In his view, Marx bases his analysis on the 'narrow legal concept of property' (Dahrendorf, 1959, p. 21ff.), whereas the correct solution is the opposite one. (This, incidentally, is a strange argument, given that much of Dahrendorf's critique of Marx concerns his alleged economism, a position which, presumably, undermines 'narrow legalism'). In Dahrendorf's view, a manager who controls has property rights because property is a 'special case of authority'. Dahrendorf, in effect, accepts Marx's quite erroneous theory of the JSC and the demise of private property associated with it, only objecting to the theme of 'classlessness' which Marx's view of progressive socialization ultimately implies. Instead, Dahrendorf proposes to 'replace the possession or non-possession of effective private property by the exercise of, or exclusion from, authority, as the criterion of class formation'. This suggests that 'control over the means of production is but a special case of authority, and the connection of control with legal property an incidental phenomenon of the industrializing societies of Europe and the US' (Dahrendorf, 1959, pp. 136–7).

The problem with Dahrendorf's analysis is, in fact, similar to that of Berle and Means except that where they divide property into two aspects (legal ownership and control), Dahrendorf turns each aspect into a discrete definition of property. Property is either theorized jn terms of legal ownership or control. Since, in his view, the latter definition is the correct one, it is clear that legal conditions, in so far as they are given any recognition at all, are simply called into being to reflect already constituted 'control' relations. Hence, the claim that the conjunction of legal ownership with control in early capitalism is simply 'incidental' or contingent. In other periods of history, including the present, control is, seemingly, subject to no effective legal conditions at all. In short, Dahrendorf's view of the law is strikingly similar to Burnham's and to that of Berle and Means.

What is equally striking, however, is that Marxists adopt a conception of the law which is substantially similar to that of their managerialist critics. Much more will be said about this when we consider the question of shareholding, but it should be clear from the earlier discussion of the JSC that Marx's conflation of individual and private property is only made possible by a dismissal of the possible effects of law. Nowhere does Marx consider the possibility that the law of incorporation might have the effect of designating the enterprise itself as economic agent of possession. Such a position is theoretically impossible for Marx, given the combination of subjective essentialism with an image of 'law as superstructure'. One important consequence of this is that Marxists have never confronted managerialism at its most fundamental conceptual level. Consequently, as we suggested above, Marxism has always had an ambiguous and problematic relationship with managerialism.

But what if one were to assume a different conception of law from that adopted by managerialists and Marxists alike? Let us assume, for example, that property ownership is always subject to legal conditions of existence, conditions which are effective in designating the possible agents which may 'possess', their capacities, rights, obligations and so on. If, for the moment, that view is accepted as legitimate, one thing becomes immediately apparent. If property relations are always subject to the effects of legal conditions of existence, the dissolution of the unity of property which constitutes the separation of ownership and control becomes impossible. The 'legal' and 'control' aspects of property can never be separated without property ceasing to exist as a meaningful relation. In short, the managerialist hypothesis collapses.

Ironically Burnham is the only writer who touches on this problem, though he does so in an entirely perverse way. In his view, since the law merely 'sums up' economic relations, the idea of a 'separation' between (legal) ownership and (factual) control is absurd: 'the concept of separation of ownership and control has no sociological or historical meaning. Ownership *means* control; if there is no control then there is no ownership' (Burnham, 1945, p. 81).

Whatever the inadequacies of Burnham's reasoning — his argument is, after all, based upon an economistic denial of the effects of law — the suggestion that ownership and control are inseparable has important repercussions. For if legal ownership and control are indeed separated, then it cannot be maintained, as Berle and Means suggest, that property is 'in transition'. The managerialist thesis implies, in effect, not just the demise of capitalist production, but of any conceivable form of economic production under the effective direction of a legally recognized category of economic agents.

What is particularly interesting is that thirty years after *The Modern Corporation and Private Property* Berle finally reaches that conclusion. Economic production is now characterized by 'power without property'. The mere separation of ownership and control is now replaced by 'something more profound — the increasing elimination of proprietary ownership itself and its replacement by, substantially, a power system' (Berle, 1960, p. 164). This argument appears to involve a recognition that the earlier attempt to distinguish between the 'active' property of managers, and the 'passive' property of shareholders is not only impossible to sustain, but largely meaningless. Why, after all, is either deemed to be property at all if one has no legal conditions of existence and the other no effectivity? The product of this recognition is a 'new social—economic structure' whose effects are 'necessarily political'; a situation where individuals participate in 'People's Capitalism' through their political influences on the democratic state.

What Berle appears to have in mind here is an economic system where the two elements which comprised the 'unity of property' have separated to such an extent that property has simply ceased to exist as an economic relation. Instead, 'control' of the means of production passes, first, into the hands of a managerial stratum and then, gradually, into the hands of the people. This peculiar conception of an economy invites several obvious questions however. First, what makes it capitalist in the absence of the domination of private property relations? Secondly, why is it an 'economic' system at all if economic relations are merely perceived as dimensions of some allegedly ubiquitous category of power? Thirdly, does 'People's Capitalism' constitute a possible form of economy? Is a system of economic production possible which does not involve property relations, either of a private or communal kind?

This last point leads us again to question the theoretical status of the very concept of 'separation' of ownership and control. The suggestion made here — so far tentatively — that possession of the means of production is sanctioned by legal conditions which have definite effects infers that managerialist theory may be conceptually incoherent. What we will now consider is the extent to which, if at all, Marxists are able to meet the sort of criticisms levelled here at managerialism.

Shareholding, corporate possession and the law

It should not be assumed that the failings noted above in Marx's analysis of the JSC are peculiar to Marx alone, a consequence of some supposed historical aberration on his part. On the contrary, it is apparent that contemporary Marxists, writing in circumstances where the corporation is the dominant economic form, are no more able to theorize corporate possession than Marx was himself. This becomes especially clear when one looks at some of the debates between Marxism and managerialism concerning shareholding and its relationship to ownership of the means of production.

It is often claimed by Marxists that top managers may be assigned to the capitalist class because they constitute the major shareholding group within the enterprise. Their 'ownership of substantial amounts of shares' combined with their 'action on behalf of capital' is said to justify this view (see, for example, *Communist Party of Great Britain*, 1978, p. 20). Now clearly Marxists do not claim that ownership of shares is a sufficient criterion for membership of the capitalist class. If this were so many wage labourers would themselves be 'capitalists' by virtue of their indirect holding of shares through pension fund investments and the like. In view of this, a distinction is usually drawn between several dimensions of

ownerships. 'Real economic ownership' (control of the means of production and the product) is distinguished from 'possession' (the ability
to put the means of production into operation) and from 'legal ownership' (see in particular Bettelheim, 1976, p. 68ff; 'real economic ownership' corresponds roughly to what has been termed 'possession' in this
text, though with two crucial qualifications; first, it is always subject to
political challenge and depends upon the achievement of relevant
political conditions for its maintenance; secondly, it always has legal
conditions of existence).

According to interpretations based upon this view (see especially
De Vroey, 1975, p. 3ff.) 'economic ownership' rests upon control of the
voting system to which legal ownership entitles participation. It therefore depends upon the holding of an amount of shares large enough to
avoid a defeat at stockholders' meetings. But legal ownership does not
automatically confer this power. That is to say, some legal owners do not
own sufficient shares to have economic ownership. This, it is claimed,
justifies the view that dispersal of stock leads, not to diffusion of economic ownership as managerialists claim, but to a concentration of it.
Marxists, from Hilferding onwards, have claimed that the dispersal of
stock leads to its antithesis — a concentration of control into fewer hands.
The greater the number of shareholders, the smaller the size of the
average holding and the smaller the proportion of total voting stock
needed for control of the enterprise. Top managers, it is said, thereby
occupy the place of capital by virtue of their large concentration of
shares. According to this position, then, legal ownership of shares cannot
guarantee 'economic ownership', but it is a necessary condition of it.

This position, however, conflates two distinct processes, the legal
ownership of shares and the legal conditions of existence of possession
(see Braverman, 1974, pp. 258–9; Carchedi, 1977, pp. 161–2; and
especially Wright, 1978, p. 76, Table 2.9., where 'legal ownership of
capital' is equated with 'stock holding'). Shareholders do not own
capital. They merely 'lend money at interest to a capital' (Cutler *et al.*,
1977, p. 155). Shareholding, in other words, is a title to wealth under
certain conditions, not a condition of possession. Legal ownership of
shares not only has to be distinguished from possession, it is generally
not a condition of existence of possession at all. An instance cited by
Poulantzas illustrates this very clearly:

> It is not necessary for a banking group to hold the majority of the share
> capital of [a] firm [legal ownership] nor even to hold any. It is often sufficient
> for the banking group simply to be selective in its financing and to differen-
> tiate in credit conditions, given the specific circumstances of the flow of
> profit, for it to impose its real control on the assignment of the means of
> production and the allocation of resources by this enterprise. (Poulantzas,
> 1975, p. 120)

The conflation of ownership of shares with the legal conditions of existence of possession is unsatisfactory because it fails to identify the dominant agent of possession under modern capitalist relations of production. What needs to be distinguished is the JSC as an entity apart from its shareholders. Marx failed to make this distinction and subsequent generations of Marxists have reproduced that failing. Contemporary theorists, like Marx, conflate agent of possession with individual by confusing legal conditions with individual forms of legal holding. This, in turn, sanctions the search for a class of individual appropriators of profit hiding behind legal forms. This is strongly suggested by Colletti's view of the modern corporation:

> The progressive *depersonalization* of property brought about the develop-
> ment of the great modern 'limited liability' company, implied the emergence
> as a *subject* of the *object* of property itself, i.e. the complete emancipation of
> property from man himself, with the result that the firm seemed to acquire
> an independent life of its own as though it were nobody's property.
> (Colletti, 1972, p. 98)

Indeed, this particular conception of the law is one which is shared by managerialists. Berle and Means, for example, quote the German writer Rathenau with approval, though his words could be mistaken for Colletti's: 'The depersonalization of ownership simultaneously implies the objecti-fication of the thing owned . . . the enterprise assumes an independent life as if it belonged to no one' (Berle and Means, 1935, p. 352).

Now this theoretical stance can lead to several possible conclusions. For instance, both Marxists and managerialists appear to regard the law as a fetish. Corporate possession is recognized, but that recognition is simultaneously denied. According to this view, the JSC hides the social (in this case essentially impersonal) relations that lie behind it. The legal conditions of existence of corporate possession are fetishized relations which obscure the true relations of production. They are the 'appearance' behind the 'essence', and in their very appearance they are effective only as a form of ideological gloss over reality. At the level of relations of production, they are entirely ineffectual (because 'superstructural'), those relations of production securing their own conditions of existence.

A similar version of this theory maintains that the corporation is somehow reducible to its constituent members (managers, shareholders, etc.). Such reducibility, it is argued, means that legal forms of recognition are mere illusions behind which 'real' persons hide. This view is one which may be held by managerialists or by Marxists. In the first case it sanctions a perusal of 'managerial behaviour', whilst in the second it justifies a search for capitalist elites or for the essential individuals for whom managers hold their powers in trust (Nichols, 1969, p. 22; Child, 1969, p. 36). What all of these positions fail to consider, however, is the possibility that capitalist relations of production may involve forms of corporate possession which are 'nobody's property'. That this may be so can be illustrated by considering the effectivity of one specific legal form, the concept of 'legal' or 'corporate personality'.

A registered company (as distinct from a partnership) is characterized by the statutory provision of 'corporate personality'. A corporation is defined according to the various Companies Acts as an association endowed with a legal personality which is separate and distinct from those of the individuals who compose it. A company is, therefore, an artificial legal person with legal rights and obligations. It is a continuing legal entity which may remain in existence irrespective of whether its members or functionaries continue to exist. It can own property, undertake contracts, sue or be sued in its own name, and be liable to tax as a company, independently of the liability of its participants. Such a legal person will employ directors who are empowered to act on its behalf, but as agents, such directors, along with all other company employees, do not have the authority to exceed the powers of the company itself.

The establishment of the corporation as a legal entity distinct from the individuals who participate in it as members, shareholders, or employees is 'not just a convenient device for the ownership of business assets . . . It also has a significant effect on the position of the members of the company, its directors and those who deal with it' (Hadden, 1972, p. 110). Three such effects are worthy of mention. First, and most obvious, is the fact that the company's separate status limits the liability of shareholders and directors. As Hadden points out, the concept of limited liability is a far-reaching one since 'a company may be convicted of a criminal offence in addition to any liability on its directors or employees, on the grounds that their acts and omissions may be attributed to the company itself' (1972, p. 111). Secondly, irrespective of the extent of managerial powers (and contrary to the view of 'sectional' managerialists and Marxists alike) managers and directors are unable to appropriate the profits of the company. Directorial remunerations are a charge against, not an appropriation of, profits. Such remunerations may, therefore, be regarded as an 'expense' (Nicholls and Carr, 1976, p. 185). Thirdly, following on from this, the company's separate legal personality means that its property must be regarded as distinct from that of its shareholders. No single shareholder, or group of shareholders, is entitled to alienate company property. One example illustrates this principle clearly:

> Gold belonging to a Dutch banking company was confiscated in 1940 by the Board of Trade as Custodian of Enemy Property, since the company fell under the terms of the definition of an enemy company. On the cessation of hostilities, the requisite sum in compensation was made over to the Administrator of Hungarian Property on the ground that all the shares were owned by Hungarians. The company itself was nonetheless ultimately

held entitled to recover the money. The company's property was 'neither the property of the shareholders nor held or managed by the company on behalf of its shareholders'; it belonged to the company alone. (Cited in Hadden, 1972, p. 112)

These facts justify a distinction being made between legal ownership of shares and the legal conditions of existence of possession. Corporate possession is sanctioned by definite forms of legal recognition. Such legal forms cannot be conceived as 'superstructural' as Marxism has conventionally argued. They do not reflect relations of production, but may satisfy certain of the conditions of existence of those relations. In doing so they will have definite substantive effects, including the separation of shareholders and functionaries, such as directors and managers, from possession. It is because Marxists have failed to give recognition to the effects of legal conditions that corporate possession has remained untheorized.

The above analysis of Marxist and managerialist approaches to law is important for several reasons. For one thing, the suggestion that legal relations can be effective in constituting non-subjective entities (corporations) as economic agents provides the basis for a conception of social agency quite different from that adopted by both sociological and Marxist traditions. For another, the mode of argument presented here implies a quite different approach to the problem of 'control' in the corporation. Both of these matters will be considered more fully in Chapter 8.

One immediate conclusion can, however, be drawn in the light of the above analysis, for it should be apparent why Marxists have failed to provide a convincing rejoinder to managerialism. The clue to this lies in the common failings of both discourses, particularly in their inability to recognize the effects of legal conditions on the constitution of economic agents. The major consequence of this is that Marxist critics of managerialism have been forced to conduct their arguments within the terrain defined by the 'separation of ownership and control'. Far from challenging the concept of 'separation', Marxists have become embroiled in debates about how much of a 'separation' can be admitted to (e.g. Miliband, 1977, p. 27). What has been suggested here, on the contrary, is that the concept of 'separation of ownership and control' is a theoretically impossible one and that, in consequence, the locus of possession under corporate capitalism is the corporation itself.

Class analysis and possession

The corporation itself constitutes the dominant form of possession in contemporary capitalism. However, corporations clearly require the function of direction to be carried out by a managerial apparatus.

Managers, in this sense, are delegated functionaries of a capital. But it is crucial to clarify what is at stake here.

It may be asked, if managers direct capital, and managerial actions constitute the decisions of enterprises, how can such enterprises be conceived as economic agents of possession? What one would appear to have here is a confirmation of the managerialist position. Management, a category of wage labour, separated from possession of the means of production, makes decisions which amount to direction (control) of the means of production. Effective control of the enterprise would appear to be in the hands of separated agents.

But the managerialist position, as we have seen, also misrecognizes the effects of legal conditions. The corporation is an agent, not because it 'takes' decisions, but because the decisions of its managerial employees are recognized by other agents and institutions as being legally ratified decisions of the enterprise. Management cannot, however, be regarded as an element of the capitalist class because of the decisions it takes. No amount of decision-making by managers grants them powers of possession of the means of production, nor any of the powers of appropriation associated with it.

This view of management and direction is very different from the Marxist one. Marxism may well recognize the manager as delegated agent, but it does so in a particular way. In De Vroey's view, for example, the separation between ownership and management refers only to 'whether the bourgeoisie itself does the job of making capital function, or whether this is done through a delegation of power' (1975, p. 4). The crucial issue here, however, is the nature of 'capital' conceived and the relationship of managerial action and decision to it. On this Marxism is quite insistent. One may regard managerial action within an individual enterprise as comprising the unit of economic decision, but the basic unit of economic *analysis* is distinct from this. To identify the latter Marxists refer back to the fundamental concepts of materialist analysis – the CMP, its laws of motion, 'capital in general', the distinction between 'essence' and 'appearance', and so on. In the case of management, then, the agent of decision (manager) is a delegate of a capital unit who realizes, by a process of 'personification', the dictates of the laws of motion of total social capital.

It is important to recognize not only how this position is theoretically sustained, but also what it implies. In classical Marxism, the 'mode of production' is regarded as a unity, or totality of levels (economic, political, ideological) with the economic level determinant in the last instance. The mode of production as unity operates according to an inbuilt, if 'contradictory' unifying principle. This principle – one which is constructed upon the materialist ontology and teleology – applies both to the mode as totality and to its constituent levels. The mode of production is a unity of unities. Each level is structured by the general principle and is placed in a conceptual hierarchy of causal relations (economic determination in the last instance), the existence of each being governed by its place in the whole. 'Capital in general' comprises one unitary element of the greater totality. Its antithesis, the working class, comprises another. At the economic level, then, capitalism comprises a totality of possessing and separated class unities. In the case of capital the implication is clear. Since the basic unit of analysis is 'capital in general', whatever may divide or distinguish individual capitals has to be regarded as secondary and peripheral.

Once the ontological and teleological principles upon which the Marxist analysis has been constructed are rejected, however, that argument collapses. If teleological laws of motion are denied, there is no reason for reducing economic agents to individuals, or groups of individuals who can 'personify' class relations. Equally, if the ontology which structures the concept of CMP is rejected, the reduction of economic relations to relations between polarized 'class unities' can no longer be sustained. However, once the conception of 'unity' is denied, the Marxist view of class, and the political objectives attached to class analysis, are called into doubt. Let us consider the problem by considering once more the Marxist concept of 'capital in general'.

To say that Marxism regards 'capital in general' as its unit of analysis is not to say that it entirely fails to recognize divisions and variations within possession. What is significant, however, is that in so far as it does recognize such variations within the 'unity of capital', it does so only within the context of attempts to assert the existence of capital as 'unity' more rigorously. Two brief examples will suffice to illustrate this.

Wright's argument (1978, ch. 2) is interesting because he does recognize possession as a relation of production which is beset by a variety of divisions. However, the direction of his analysis is, in turn, governed by the fundamental theoretical assumption of the Marxist analysis — that classes of possessing and separated agents comprise unities at root. Wright, therefore, sets variations within possession/separation in the context of the political objective of class analysis. In this view, the bourgeoisie and proletariat may be designated as agents of possession and separation in a relatively unproblematic way. Variations within possession/separation may then be fitted into a continuum between these polarized unities. The fact that the majority of positions within the social division of labour are placed in the continuum does not alter the fact that Wright's assumption is consistent with the view that classes are unities, for it is only their relation to one or other class unity that defines them as 'contradictory class locations'. Wright's recognition of variations within possession is undermined by the political project he sets himself; to establish variations as locations within polarized class unities. Such positions can only be considered 'contradictory' because of the assumption that, at the most general level, classes are unities whose unity is expressed in polarized forms of politics. Thus, 'contradictory class locations' are positions in the social division of labour which are, more or less, bourgeois (capitalist in political orientation) or proletarian (socialist).

Though Poulantzas's examination of 'contradictions within the bourgeoisie' (1975, pt 2) also recognizes divisions within capital, it is based upon the same theoretical assumptions as Wright's position. Divisions within the class of possessors are examined within the context of a model of polarized class unities: 'the forms of contradiction among the dominant classes and fractions always depend on the forms of the principal contradiction, which is that between the bourgeoisie as a whole and the working class' (Poulantzas, 1975, p. 107).

A large part of Poulantzas's discussion is directed towards an historical examination of the 'dissociations' between the elements of capitalist relations of production (economic ownership, possession, legal ownership) in the setting of the transition from competitive to monopoly capitalism. There are a variety of political purposes behind this discussion. For example, Poulantzas's stated intention is to reject both those political positions which regard non-monopoly capital as sufficiently divorced from its monopoly counterpart to constitute a political ally of the working class, and those which regard capital as an integrated totality.

Political considerations apart, the discussion is a lengthy one and for present purposes a brief example will suffice (Poulantzas, 1975, pp. 146–7). Poulantzas argues that in the current phase of monopoly capitalism there has been a progressive (though by no means uniform or unilinear) loss of 'economic ownership' and 'possession' by non-monopoly capital vis-à-vis monopoly capital. Behind the legal façade of retained independent ownership the boundaries of enterprises are being dissolved. Many enterprises are, in effect, dependent production units that form part of more complex units. Under such conditions, conglomerates determine many of the conditions of production of subsidiaries.

Now much of what Poulantzas indicates is empirically defensible, and he rightly suggests that there are, consequently, considerable variations within possession. 'Possession' is not, in fact, an all-or-nothing category, since certain categories of possessor may be effectively separated from certain of their conditions of production.

What is significant about Poulantzas's approach, however, is that such 'dissociations' can only be understood in relation to the teleology of 'monopoly capitalism' from which they derive. Whatever particular significance such dissociations may have, the crucial point for Poulantzas is that they are divisions within capital, rather than between capitals. They are, in effect, a necessary consequence of the fact that 'capital in general' realizes monopolistic tendencies. Divisions within capital are only possible then, *because* of the unity which constitutes capital. They are forms of appearance of an inner essence, the laws of motion of the CMP, such laws being effected through 'capital as unity'. What is significant in both examples is that in neither case is the 'unity of capital' considered to have any determinate conditions of existence. The basic unity of classes of possessing and separated agents is given in the structuring mechanism of the capitalist totality. 'Capital' has a unity which derives from its position within the structure of the CMP. The unity or 'general interest' of capital is not a product of political compromises between capitals, nor of organized alliances with political agencies. It has no social or political conditions of production. The mere identification of economic classes seemingly guarantees their constitution as unities at some allegedly 'fundamental' level. This, in turn, sanctions a reading of politics, law, ideology and culture in 'class' terms.

The suggestion here, however, is that in the absence of teleology and ontology, 'capital as unity' can no longer provide a basis for the analysis of possession. The relevant unit of analysis has to be capitals, not capital, since the unity of capitals cannot merely be assumed. This is not to say that capitals cannot achieve degrees of unity. It is merely to recognize that there may be serious divisions within capital which socialists, having identified, may exploit. Moreover, where some degree of unity is realized by sections of capital, the forms which that unity may take, its scope and stability, will depend upon the production and reproduction of definite social and political conditions. Such unity is not inevitable and its existence in any particular context implies no necessary destiny for capitalism.

Marxism, Politics and the State

4

Classical Marxism and the state

In this chapter and the following one we concentrate on the Marxist theory of the state, paying particular attention to analyses of the capitalist state. State theory will be examined here with particular reference to its strategic relevance in socialist political calculation. The present chapter will attempt to outline some of the central themes and issues found in classical versions of Marxist state theory. For our purposes 'classical' will refer here to the works of Marx, Engels, Lenin and Gramsci. Our intention is not to provide a 'summary' of classical state theory — far less a definitive one — but to isolate certain central issues and problems. The matters which are isolated here will be reconsidered in Chapter 5, this time in the context of some of the modern versions of Marxist state theory.

A correct analysis of the state is of obvious importance for Marxism. The state, after all, constitutes one of the objects towards which socialist political practice is invariably directed. This much can be verified by considering some of the problems which Marxism has continuously posed. What is the effectiveness of 'reformist' strategies towards the state? What are the characteristics of state action with respect to capital? What are the limits and possibilities of 'statist' versions of socialism? In short, the state has always comprised a crucial strategic object for analysis. Indeed, in Lenin's words 'the key question of every revolution is undoubtedly the question of state power' (1917a, p. 366).

Our concern in these two chapters is to consider whether state theory, which is, after all, regarded as a critical strategic exercise by Marxists, gives any clear direction to socialist strategy vis-à-vis the state. It will be suggested that far from providing an adequate strategy, the main body of state theory fails to provide even the pre-conditions of a potentially effective political practice. This failure will be traced to a number of inadequacies, not least of which is an alarming failure to identify the strategic object, 'the state', with any degree of precision.

Proponents of Marxist state theory might retort that it is precisely this project with which that theory is concerned. Indeed, they may claim that such a project is more or less successfully realized by much of the literature which has emerged in the last decade. What will be suggested here, however, is that that literature and the classical formulations on the state which precede it are fundamentally incoherent. This incoherence arises as a necessary consequence of the 'materialist conception of politics', variations of which all Marxists adopt. According to this conception 'politics' is an element of the social formation whose structure is an effect of its place in a material hierarchy of 'levels' or 'forms'. Ultimately, politics may be regarded as a process of 'class conflict', the basic agents of political practice being classes which have objectively defined and antagonistic 'class interests'. These interests constitute the basis of different forms of political structure and practice.

Marxism's insistence on the priority of such a materialist analysis is combined, however, with a 'recognition' of the irreducibility of political apparatuses and practices. On the one hand, the state has to be regarded as fundamentally an 'expression' of capitalist relations of production, and in that sense reducible. On the other hand, because it is recognized that a realization of the 'specificity' of politics is of crucial strategic and practical significance, such 'reductionism' has to be theoretically tempered. Marxist theory attempts to make these differing views of politics compatible by subjecting materialist forms of determination to varying degrees of 'complexity' so that the relationship of economic classes and politics may be regarded as 'relatively autonomous', 'dialectical', and the like.

It is suggested here that these arguments are incoherent. Indeed, the real issue that has escaped Marxist discussion concerns not whether Marxism is 'reductionist' but whether it is coherent. Marxists have *only* been able to make (in some cases) effective interventions in politics *because* of their non-reductionist 'recognition' of the specific conditions of political 'conjunctures'. That Marxism has generally 'recognized' ideological, cultural, or national conditions in political calculation is not a matter of dispute. The problem is the theoretical status of such 'recognitions'. Can one, in other words, make the theoretical concepts of materialism compatible with the 'non-reductionist' forms of recognition that Marxists give to politics? The two chapters which we devote to state theory suggest that an affirmative response to that question is ruled out by virtue of the basic incoherence of the materialist position.

The state and class domination

Marx and Engels

The beginnings of the materialist analysis of politics can be traced to the formulations of the *German Ideology* of 1846. Though Marx had written on politics and the state before this, the earliest views were abandoned — notably the Hegelian notion of the 'ideal state' — and even where the earlier writings tried to establish connections between the state and class relations this was done in a relatively simplistic manner. For example, the 1842 articles on the 'wood thefts' suggest a strong connection between private interests and state legislation, but at this stage the problem is considered to be the 'prostitution' of the state to private interests, a proposition which is still considered to reveal the gap between the state as reality and the state as ideal (Draper, 1977, p. 71).

The attempt to link the state and politics with class domination in a more rigorous and systematic way emerges in the *German Ideology*. Here Marx and Engels attempt to set politics in a materialist context of determinate relations of production:

> The social structure and the state are continually evolving out of the life-processes of definite individuals, but of individuals, not as they may appear in their own or other people's imagination, but as they *really* are; i.e., as they operate, produce materially, and hence as they work under definite material limits, presuppositions and conditions independent of their will. (1846, p. 24)

Above all else, the theme of the historical specificity of such 'material conditions', and thus of their corresponding state forms, is crucial to the Marxian analysis, distancing it from other theories of the state. For Marxism denies that there are any 'universal' political or state functions and refuses to conceive the state as an inevitable product of social differentiation and complexity. Indeed, Lenin, writing before most sociological theories of the state were formulated is dismissive of those views which rest upon 'a few phrases borrowed from Spencer or Mikhailovsky, by referring to the growing complexity of social life, the differentiation of functions and so forth' (Lenin, 1917b, p. 11).

Instead, in Engels's view, it is emphasized that the state is a product of society at a 'certain stage of development', the stage of the beginnings of the social division of labour, private property, the emergence of classes and the antagonisms which accompany such an emergence (1884, p. 576). Each state is specific to a determinate historical class structure and form of extraction of surplus labour in this view. In ancient times it is 'the state of the slave owning citizens; in the middle ages, the feudal lords; in our own, the bourgeoisie' (Engels, 1880, p. 424).

The important point for Marx and Engels is that the state, far from being universal, is a *'special'* institution appearing in conjunction with the emergence of classes. It is because materialism maintains that the emergence of classes inevitably gives rise to antagonistic class interests, that the state is considered to be a special coercive apparatus for the maintenance of the interests of the dominant class. Whereas social order in 'primitive communism' is regarded as a function of the community as a whole, in a society based upon classes with mutually antagonistic interests the conflicts which arise can only be resolved by the formation of a special apparatus that is both 'an expression of the social power' of the dominant class (Marx and Engels, 1846, p. 40) and a condition of its continued dominance. Engels argues that

> In order that these antagonisms and classes with conflicting economic interests might not consume themselves and society in fruitless struggle, it became necessary to have a power seemingly standing above society that would alleviate the conflict, and keep it within the bounds of 'order'; and this power . . . is the state. (1884, p. 576)

One can see in all this the rudiments of a materialist theory of the state, for already Marx and Engels have a conception of it as an historically specific apparatus, occupying the place of a special institution in society, whose function is to maintain the interests of a dominant class. Indeed, certain of their comments are suggestive of themes developed more thoroughly by later Marxists. Engels's view of the state as a power standing 'apparently above society' is, for example, indicative of both modern theories of the state as 'fetish' and of the state as 'factor of cohesion'.

Nevertheless, one can already see the emergence of theoretical dilemmas which survive up to the present. One such dilemma concerns the concept of 'class domination' itself, for Marx and Engels invoke a conception of the state as superstructure combined with a recognition that the state provides certain conditions of existence of a dominant class's capacity to 'dominate'. In this instance the state is conceived both as 'effect' of material conditions, and as 'effective' in their constitution. In its effective mode the state's institutions are involved in the 'organization of . . . the exploiting class for the maintenance of its external conditions of production' (Engels, 1876–8, p. 332). But, at the same time, Marx and Engels insist that institutional forms of politics, however effective they may appear, are elements of a more fundamental essence; 'all struggles within the state, the struggles for the franchise, etc., etc., are merely the illusory forms in which the real struggles of the different classes are fought out among one another' (1846, p. 35). In this case we are presented with a view of social relations in which agents both personify class relations (so that capitalist laws of motion are realized 'independently of the will' of individual agents) and misrecognize the real.

This view of social agency assumes a fundamental distinction between 'essence' and 'appearance'. One of the most crucial arguments of the *German Ideology* concerns the view that the reproduction of class relations is itself dependent upon the essential processes of production being 'estranged' by the act of misrecognition on the part of social agents, so that they appear as 'an objective power above us, growing out of our control' (Marx and Engels, 1846, p. 36). The duality of personification/misrecognition is, therefore, seen as a necessary condition for the reproduction of class relations, a view which gives rise in contemporary debates to the state being conceived as a 'fetishized form' of social relations.

What this particular example suggests is that we have to examine the problem of the relationship of sets of assumptions within Marxist discourse. Can one, for instance, provide an adequate theoretical solution to Marx and Engels's recognition of the effectivity of state institutions by conceiving such effectivity as a mere fetish? What one is posing here, in effect, is the question of internal consistency and coherence within the Marxist conceptual scheme.

This problem is a recurrent one within Marxist discourse, occurring at a number of levels of analysis. Many writers, for example, have recognized the need for Marxism to be able to marry its general theory of the CMP to the specific analysis of political structures and practices in particular social formations (the so-called problem of 'specificity'). At the level of the capitalist state, the tension between the 'general' and the 'particular' has been apparent. Jessop observes that Marxists have tended to eschew attempts to analyse the state as a set of institutions, since this clashes with the view of society as a 'totality' composed of 'levels' in a more or less complex relationship (1982, p. 22). Those Marxists who have, rightly, seen the need to perceive the state as a set of institutions producing definite effects have, consequently, been constrained by the very assumptions that define the materialist mode of analysis. The result has been a rather crude 'instrumentalism'. Miliband's solution is a fairly typical one. The state is conceived as a non-unitary totality whose institutions enjoy a relative autonomy (specificity) that may produce determinate effects. But that specificity is denied by the view that state institutions represent a class which itself constitutes a unitary totality. Marxism's reluctance to provide a rigorous institutional analysis leaves us with a niggling question which refuses to go away. Where is the state?

This instance is, as we have suggested, part of a wider problem of how to relate the general and the specific. It is significant that a recent addition to the Marxist theory of politics and the state pays considerable attention to precisely this question. The manner in which Jessop approaches the problem is interesting since he suggests that there is no 'Marxian theory of the state', Marx and Engels producing several versions of state theory which differ according to the particular problems that they address. Moreover, he maintains that there cannot be a single materialist theory of the state 'without rejecting the basic premises of historical materialism' (Jessop, 1982, p. 29). What Marxists can aim for, however, is an abstract (general) theory of the state which can be complemented by an analysis of multiple determinations to produce a theory of concrete (specific) states by the 'method of articulation'.

Though Jessop is clearly aware of the issues at stake his approach raises an obvious question about the theoretical objects 'state theory' and 'historical materialism'. To put it bluntly, if it is to be maintained that Marx and Engels's 'discontinuity' precludes a general theory of the state, why should we assume that historical materialism itself constitutes a relatively coherent unity, a continuous object whose 'basic premises' condition Marxist discourse in certain pre-determined directions so that any contravention of those premises amounts to a break with 'Marxism'? For what we shall suggest in due course is that the basic premises and concepts of Marxism leave sufficient space for manoeuvre to generate a state of theoretical indeterminacy in political discourse. Witness, for example, the problems which arise in attempting to interpret Marx's own writings in a political or strategic context. Gramsci's article *The Revolution Against 'Capital'* is rife with confusion about whether historical materialism *is* economistic, or whether it has merely been contaminated by economism. The correct answer to this problem − that Marxism is both, and much more besides − cannot be contemplated in a position which reduces Marxist theoretical discourse and, indeed, political practice, to the effect of certain basic concepts. These matters will be considered again in our final assessment of reductionism.

Returning to the 'class domination' view of the state which we outlined above, it is necessary to extract two points for further consideration. In the first place, if the state is a mere form of representation of class interests, it follows that the state apparatus cannot be regarded as a politically neutral medium vis-à-vis the interests it represents. There is, therefore, a persistent injunction in the political writings of classical Marxists which demands the 'smashing' of the state apparatus in any serious revolutionary initiative. At the same time, however, even though the state comprises 'a committee for managing the common affairs of the whole bourgeoisie' (Marx and Engels, 1848, pp. 110−11) the particular differences of interest which arise within such 'common affairs' are deemed to rule out the view of the state as a simple 'instrument' of capital. It is to these two issues that attention will now be turned. We shall first consider, briefly, the strategic imperative to 'smash' the state. Then we shall examine in rather more detail the problem of the so-called 'relative autonomy' of the capitalist state.

'Smashing the state apparatus'

The earliest verification of the need for any successful revolution to smash the existing state apparatus is, in the view of Marx and Engels, offered by the experiences of the Paris Commune, which showed that 'the working class cannot simply lay hold of the ready made state machinery, and wield it for its own purposes' (1848, p. 99).

This same imperative for a successful socialist revolution to smash the state apparatus is at the centre of Lenin's position; indeed, he takes the view that such an imperative necessarily follows from the materialist analysis. It is the adoption of this political position which, for him, distinguishes Marxism from the 'reformism' of those who seek to achieve a socialist transformation by parliamentary means, a position which, in Lenin's view, fails to identify 'bourgeois democracy' as a form of state which, whatever benefits it might offer to the working class, provides the 'best possible political shell for capitalism' (Lenin, 1970c, p. 15).

Contrary to this view, and in accordance with the pronouncements of Marx and Engels, Lenin argues that a transformation of capitalist relations of production requires a destruction of their very conditions of existence, which are provided by the class powers embedded in the state. He rightly points out that this much is asserted in Marx's letter to Weydemeyer of 1852, which argues '(1) that the existence of classes is only bound up with particular phases in the development of production, (2) that class struggle necessarily leads to the dictatorship of the prolet-ariat' (1852b, p. 528). In other words, it is asserted that the transition period between capitalism and socialism will itself be characterized by a 'class struggle' and the imposition of a new form of state, 'the dictator-ship of the proletariat', an act which will itself involve the destruction of the bourgeois state apparatus.

A clear account of what this might imply for socialist strategy in parliamentary democracies is contained in Lenin's pamphlet *Left-Wing Communism*. Here Lenin rejects the 'ultra-leftist' denial of all parliamentary political activity, arguing instead for a severely restricted use of parlia-mentary democratic institutions. In practice, what this amounts to is the utilization of democratic institutions for the purposes of agitation and propaganda. This view rests upon the suggestion that parliamentary democracy is politically 'obsolete' and 'ineffectual' (Lenin, 1917b, p. 42), but that because its obsolescence is not fully recognized by the masses, it must be 'supported'. Lenin, however, conceives this support of parliamentary institutions and reformist politicians in a particularly restricted sense: 'I want to support Henderson [parliamentary democracy] in the same way as a rope supports a hanged man' (1917b, p. 71). The political objective of this strategy of support and participation is to expose and discredit the institutions of the bourgeois state, and by so doing, to reveal them as bourgeois, whilst simultaneously raising the conscious-ness of the masses. Lenin, therefore, advocates the use of parliamentary means to 'disintegrate parliament from within' though without in any sense advocating a parliamentary road to socialist transition.

The fact that the strategy advocated by Lenin for use in parliamentary democracies such as Britain was entirely ineffective is a matter of historical fact. But there are broader problems relating to the coherence of the general strategy of 'smashing the state apparatus', two of which, for the moment, may merely be noted. First, the assumption that parliamentary democratic institutions are 'obsolete' is not only a piece of wishful thinking, but a failure to recognize both the conditions which such institutions provide for the reproduction of capitalist relations, and the possibilities they might offer for transforming them. Secondly, the call to smash the state *in toto* implies that state institutions comprise a cohesive and unitary totality whose effects are general rather than particular. This image, we shall suggest, is both theoretically and strategically naive.

The relative autonomy of the capitalist state

Marx and Engels

Although the call for a 'smashing' of the bourgeois state rests upon conceiving it as primarily an apparatus of class domination, Marxism also consistently maintains that the state is not merely class reducible, but that it possesses a degree of independence or 'relative autonomy'. One can find general indications of this in the classical writings, such as Engels's claim that 'on the whole, the economic movement gets its way, but it has also to suffer reactions from the political movement which it itself established and endowed with relative independence' (1890, p. 686).

By far the clearest exposition of the state's relative autonomy is, however, usually considered to be found in Marx's analysis of the political conditions in France, and to a lesser extent, those in Germany and Britain. The argument presented in *The Class Struggles in France 1848–50*, for example, sets out to show that political domination is not exercised by a homogeneous ruling class, but by factions of the bourgeoisie in more or less temporary coalition. In contrast to the July Monarchy of Louis Philippe which was dominated by the financial faction of the bourgeoisie, the period of the Second Republic is dominated by a coalition between, on the one hand the finance aristocracy and the big bourgeoisie (represented by the Orleanists), and on the other, the landed nobility (represented by the Legitimists). The Provisional Government which emerged after the February Revolution was a compromise between mutually antagonistic interests, but it was a compromise which, in Marx's view, enabled the factions united in the 'Party of Order' to maintain their 'common class interests without giving up their mutual rivalry' (Marx, 1850, p. 251). More than this, it was able 'to complete the rule of the bourgeoisie, by allowing, beside the finance aristocracy, all the propertied classes to enter the orbit of political power' (Marx, 1850, p. 212).

Marx follows a related theme in his later text on the period leading up to the coup of 1851, *The Eighteenth Brumaire of Louis Bonaparte*, when he argues that the Bonapartist state 'seems' to have become independent, though, in fact, it bears a complex relationship of representation to various classes, this fact being said to explain the contradictions of the government (Marx, 1852a, pp. 484–5). On the one hand Bonapartism represents, or at least appears to represent, the small holding peasantry. On the other hand, the regime effectively functions to 'safeguard bourgeois order': 'it was the only form of government possible at a time when the bourgeoisie had already lost and the working class had not yet acquired the faculty of ruling the nation' (Marx, 1871, pp. 286–7).

There is a strong suggestion here, not only that the bourgeoisie is peculiarly incapable of leading its own revolution (for commentary on this see Poulantzas, 1973b, p. 183; Draper, 1977, p. 321ff.), but also that relative autonomy serves to permit the state to obey its 'class role' more effectively. Draper's comment on Engels's analysis of the Bismarckian state makes this point clearly:

> The autonomy . . . was strictly relative. For its success was conditional on the fact that its policy was really in the basic interests of the ruling classes and that this fact could be demonstrated before too long. (1977, p. 328; see also Miliband, 1977, p. 87)

Marx and Engels's comment on Britain is based upon very much the same assumptions:

> The Whigs are the aristocratic representatives of the bourgeoisie, of the industrial and commercial middle class. Under the conditions that the bourgeoisie should abandon to them an oligarchy of aristocratic families, the monopoly of government and the exclusive possession of office, they make to the middle class, and assist it in conquering all those concessions which in the course of social and political developments have shown them-selves to have become unavoidable and undelayable. (1852, p. 330)

The suggestion is, then, that political outcomes reflect the structural dictates of the materialist teleology — the class interests of 'capital in general', under the direction of capitalist laws of development. The theme that the state's separation or relative autonomy only underlines its capacity to represent the interests of total social capital above and beyond particular interests is an instance of what is referred to in the *German Ideology*, as the state giving the bourgeoisie 'a general form to its mean average interests' (Marx and Engels, 1846, p. 77).

Gramsci, hegemony and the modern state

Amongst classical theorists, it is without doubt in the work of Gramsci that one finds the most sustained and theoretically sophisticated attempt to conceive the state and politics as a relatively autonomous level of the social totality. In view of this we shall pay particular attention to his work for much of the remainder of this chapter.

It is apparent that the connecting theme of much of Gramsci's work was that of 'economism'. In his view, the problem of economism was a theoretical question which had fundamental practical relevance. As such it had to be contested, both in theory and practice, as 'primitive infantilism' (Gramsci, 1971, p. 407).

The rationale for this project of defeating economism in theory and practice is a simple one. Economistic theory, it is assumed, leads to errors in political practice. In consequence, a great deal of Gramsci's work is devoted to examining the alleged practical effects of economistic theory. The political events of the postwar period merely underlined for him the fact that economistic and catastrophic theories of capitalist breakdown were untenable. Indeed, Gramsci depicts the 1917 Revolution as a *Revolution Against 'Capital'*, an occasion where 'events have overcome ideologies' (1977, p. 34).

In this example, we are presented with a rudimentary statement of elements which later develop into a more refined theory; the period leading up to the Revolution is an 'abnormal' one; the crisis which arises is built on the back of war, famine and socialist propaganda which, together, 'forged the people's will'. In other words, he identifies an 'exceptional' period of crisis, where specific national and international conditions produce an event which exceeds the parameters of 'normal' political development.

Gramsci's work has to be situated, therefore, in the political circumstances of the period; the postwar crisis; the emergence of fascism in Italy; the organization of the Italian Communist Party (PCI) and the policy of the Comintern towards fascism. Many writers are, in view of this, keen to emphasize the extent to which Gramscian theory can be directly attributed to his struggle against 'economistic practice'. Buci-Glucksmann, for example, conceives the theoretical writings of the late 1920s and early 1930s as a direct response to the economism of the Comintern's 'Third Period' (1980, pp. 242–3). The same author regards Gramsci as the first Marxist to challenge the mechanistic base/superstructure model of politics and the state at both theoretical and practical levels simultaneously, an advance made possible by the concept of 'hegemony'. Contrary to some writers, she maintains that Gramsci is far more than simply a theorist of the ideological dimension who supplements the Leninist theory of the state as 'domination and repression'. Instead, it is argued that Gramsci provides a rigorous re-drafting of Marxist state theory, and is, in effect, the foremost Marxist theorist of 'the political' (see also Boggs, 1976, p. 12).

Having said that, the interpretation of Gramsci as a theorist of 'the political' has been controversial. Part of this has been due to the abstraction of much of his 'prison' writing, though some of it is due to theoretical 'imperialism' between the various schools of Marxist thought. (Compare Bobbio's attempt to depict Gramsci as a Marxist humanist with Texier's view of him as a theorist of the superstructure; in Mouffe, 1979).

The core of Gramsci's work is usually associated with the concept of hegemony, a term referring to a relation between classes and fractions of classes where one group exercises leadership over another by gaining active consent. Hegemony is, then, a relation, not of domination by force, but of consent by means of 'intellectual and moral leadership'.

It is notable — especially in view of the way 'instrumentalist' writers, such as Miliband, have used the concept — that Gramsci relates the concept both to bourgeois and proletarian classes. In an article of 1923 entitled *What Is To Be Done?* Gramsci gives an explanation for the defeat of the revolutionary parties in Italy; 'our weakness . . . is . . . not to have had an ideology; not to have disseminated it among the masses; not to have strengthened the consciousness of their militants with certitudes of a moral and psychological character' (1978, p. 171). But, equally, he depicts the Risorgimento as having failed at the ideological level to weld the population into a national community, the Piedmontese ruling class having merely established 'domination without leadership: dictatorship without hegemony' (Gramsci, 1971, p. 106). In both instances it is clear that Gramsci sees the establishment of hegemony as a necessary condition of the effective functioning of any regime or organization, whether it be bourgeois or proletarian.

The struggle for the establishment of hegemony amounts, then, to a pre-condition of an effective socialist politics. One key area in all of this will, of course, concern the question of 'moral and psychological' leadership and, in particular, the types of issues around which popular hegemony might be organized. It is striking — though hardly surprising, given the fascist context in which Gramsci was writing — that he is one of the few Marxists to pay serious attention to the concept of 'nation' as an object, both of political theory and popular mobilization. In consequence, he insists that although Marxists need to adopt an international perspective, such internationalism can only be made realistic by invoking a national dimension. Moreover 'it is in the concept of hegemony that exigencies which are national in character are knotted together' (Gramsci, 1971, p. 241). The Party's point of departure must, therefore, be a national one and its analysis must be, first and foremost, adequate in a national context. In this respect Gramsci insists that an effective socialist politics has, as a necessary and legitimate component, the objective of mobilizing support on a 'national—popular' basis.

It is apparent that Gramsci sees the concept of hegemony as an historically specific one, one thing to which he draws attention being the variable
relationship between state and civil society in different periods and
locations. In Russia, it is suggested, 'the state was everything' whilst
civil society 'was primordial and gelatinous'. This contrasts with the
situation in the West where, it is said, the state was only an 'outer ditch'
behind which stood a developed civil society (Gramsci, 1971, p. 238).
This distinction gives rise to possible implications in two spheres. At the
level of theory, it might be assumed that work on hegemony in the modern
state needs to be undertaken to complement the classical Leninist
analysis found in *State and Revolution*. At the level of practice, it might be
supposed that such an analysis will suggest new forms of strategy for
dealing with the problem of the state. In fact, Gramsci's work develops in
both of these directions.

One important element of Gramsci's analysis concerns the way in
which he draws conceptual refinements and political conclusions from
the distinction between 'state' and 'civil society'. Since this distinction is
at the basis of his development of the concept of hegemony, it is obviously
crucial that it is drawn rigorously and coherently.

In fact, Gramsci's use of these concepts is more complicated than it
might first appear to be. Showstack Sassoon, for example, observes that
he dispenses with the traditional Marxist schema where 'political' and
'ideological' levels of the superstructure occupy different theoretical
spaces. Instead, parts of the state machinery, or institutions like the church,
can occupy two spaces simultaneously, as dimensions of both political
and civil society. In her view, 'any division is purely methodological'
(Showstack Sassoon, 1980, p. 112), a view also put forward by Togliatti
(1979, pp. 203–5), who insists that there is a crucial political lesson to be
learned from the fact that Gramsci attributes a 'methodological' rather
than an 'organic' value to the state/civil society distinction. For what this
indicates is that any class seeking political power needs to carry out the
struggle for hegemony at different levels of society, in varying ways,
according to particular circumstances. Writers sympathetic to the
Gramscian view suggest that this methodological starting point (state/
civil society) creates a potential for far more varied forms of political
intervention by socialists than are permitted by other writers in the
Marxist tradition. In short, Gramsci's 'expanded' definition of the state
and politics creates space for a fuller conception of socialist political
practice and socialist transformation.

Some justification for this view can be found in other basic concepts in
Gramscian analysis. Most notable is the concept of the 'integral' state
itself where we are presented with the formula 'State = political society
+ civil society, in other words hegemony protected by the armour of
coercion' (Gramsci, 1971, p. 263). The methodological distinction upon

which this definition is constructed provides the basis for a set of related dualisms which are intended to have implications for theory and strategy. For example, the political society/coercion and civil society/hegemony pair are reflected in another pair of concepts at the level of social transformation. Here, Gramsci distinguishes 'conjunctural' and 'organic' conditions, the former referring to the immediate political terrain and the forces involved therein, the latter referring to longer term structural trends. Confusion in analysing the relative effects of these conditions can lead to an excess of 'economism' or 'ideologism', we are told, though the 'dialectical nexus' between the two makes precise analysis difficult (Gramsci, 1971, p. 178).

The distinction between long term and short term conditions is likewise reflected at the level of socialist strategy. Here, Gramsci draws an important distinction between 'war of manoeuvre' and 'war of position'. By the former he refers to a 'frontal attack' on the state, a stage of politics which relates, broadly speaking, to periods of acute 'conjunctural' crisis. One is dealing here with matters of force and military confrontation. However, Gramsci's basic strategic proposition is that long term ideological struggle − a 'war of position' − will become increasingly important to socialist politics in modern capitalist societies where one is confronted by an 'integral state'.

The concept of 'war of position' has a crucial place in Gramsci's theory. For one thing, it is, on the strategic level, an attempt to correct the error of economism. For another, on the theoretical level it is closely interwoven with the concept of hegemony. Indeed, in an early formulation Gramsci comments that 'the war of position in politics, is the concept of hegemony' (cited in Showstack Sassoon, 1980, p. 197). Finally, the concept has far-reaching implications for the way in which socialist transformation of society is to be conceived, since Gramsci apparently sees the 'war of position' as the decisive revolutionary stage over and above the 'war of manoeuvre':

> the 'war of position', once won, is won definitively. In politics, in other words, the war of manoeuvre subsists so long as it is a question of winning positions which are not decisive . . . But when, for one reason or another, these positions have lost their value and only the decisive positions are at stake, then one passes over to siege warfare. (1971, p. 239)

The suggestion here is that the struggle for hegemony is long and protracted, both sides in the struggle 'digging in' for a state of siege. More significantly, however, it is suggested that the struggle for hegemony will be decisive both before and after the revolutionary process is under way. The very process of socialist transformation is, so to speak, one involving hegemonic struggle. This is precisely the point of the comment which follows the 'integral' definition of the state, Gramsci suggesting that such a definition is fundamental to any doctrine of the state which 'conceives the latter as tendentially capable of withering away and of being subsumed into regulated society' (1971, p. 263). What is being proposed here is that a struggle for hegemony will take place after the seizure of the state, whose effects will shape the nature of 'regulated civil society' which exists under socialism. It is obvious, then, that Gramsci sees socialist transformation as more of a 'process' than an 'event'.

Some major themes and issues

Finally, let us isolate some of the major themes which arise in the 'classical' analysis of the state, our intention here being to identify problems which, though arising in the classical works, endure in those contemporary analyses to be discussed in Chapter 5.

(1)   The first and most basic problem is indicated in Engels's claim that the state is 'as a rule, the state of the most powerful, economically dominant class, which *through the medium of the state*, becomes also the politically dominant class' (Engels, 1884, pp. 577−8 emphasis added). Political power and domination are here conceived to be conditional upon access to the 'medium of the state'. That medium is, in effect, the condition of the dominant class becoming politically dominant, for without the conditions of production of political power provided by the state there can be no power. For Marx and Engels, then, the state produces necessary conditions and in so doing generates definite effects.

Yet, at the same time, Marxism also conceives the state as an expression of already constituted class powers. In *The German Ideology* the state is viewed as an 'expression' of the 'social power' which is derived from property ownership (Marx and Engels, 1846, p. 40). This image seems to imply a denial of the effectivity of the medium of the state in the constitution of 'power'. A class's power is, in this case, assumed to be unconditional, an effect of the structure of the CMP, rather than a product of political conditions. According to this view the state may be regarded as an 'expression', a 'reflection' or a 'personification' of the economy. In Engels's view, for example, it is 'the ideal personification of the total national capital' (1876−8, p. 330).

In the following chapter we shall consider how these inconsistencies are reproduced in modern state theory and the consequences they have.

(2)   This first question raises the problem of how the concept of 'class power' is theorized in Marxist discourse. One major debating point in contemporary state theory has concerned the way in which 'class power' and 'state power' should be distinguished (Miliband, 1973, p. 88). Though many Marxists recognize that such a distinction has to be

rigorously maintained if a concept such as 'relative autonomy' is to be defended, we suggest below that much of this work is problematic. Indeed, in the following four chapters, we shall suggest that the problem is not just one of theorizing 'class power' as opposed to 'state power', but of querying the concepts of 'class', 'state' and 'power' as constituted in Marxist discourse.

(3)   These matters are closely related to the problem of connecting the general with the specific. All Marxists recognize this as a crucial question and those who have engaged in practical struggles have regarded a solution to it as fundamental to effective political intervention. We have already seen that Gramsci was pre-occupied with the matter in connection with the 'national' question. The same is true of Lenin:

> the task consists in learning to apply the general and the basic principles of communism to the *specific* relations between classes and parties, to the *specific features* in the objective development towards communism, which are different in each country . . . To seek out, investigate, predict and grasp that which is nationally specific. (Lenin, 1920b, pp. 72 and 75)

But the problem is that such 'specificity of condition' is circumscribed by materialist ontology and teleology, the problematic effects of which have already been seen in our discussion of the economy.

(4)   In raising again the issues of ontology and teleology we are indicating an enduring problem. Marxism has tried to temper the effects of ontology (politics as 'superstructural') and teleology (political outcomes as determined rather than determinate) by invoking the concepts of 'relative autonomy' and 'dialectics'. It is clear, for example, that Gramsci, for one, tries to lay down the basis for a non-reductionist Marxism which has the capacity to recognize the specificity of social relations. In this regard his work can be seen as a deliberate attempt to challenge cruder varieties of Marxism by seeking a re-formulation of the 'base' versus 'superstructure' dichotomy and by producing a non-teleological theory which allows room for such 'specifics' as 'errors of calculation' on the part of political leaders (Gramsci, 1971, p. 408). However laudable these objectives might be, there remains the question of whether the solutions proposed are theoretically coherent. In the following chapters we subject some of these solutions (relative autonomy and the like) to sustained criticism and suggest that they are both theoretically untenable and strategically empty.

(5)   Our discussion of Gramsci raises another serious question regarding Marxist definitions of the object 'the state'. Whatever the strategic benefits of the 'expanded' or 'integral' definition of the state are alleged to be, Gramsci, like all Marxists, has an astonishing reluctance to isolate the boundaries of the state in any precise way. We shall see in the following chapter that Marxism vacillates between narrow views of the

state (the state as a nebulous entity which embodies certain functions) and very broad ones (the state as a complex of institutions and practices whose presence is socially ubiquitous).

(6)   Finally, there remains the question of 'economism' or 'reductionism' itself. We have already observed that much of the rationale for producing a rigorous state theory lies in the attempt to combat the effects of economism. But are we to assume, with Gramsci, that the effects of economistic theory are revealed in economistic practice? All Marxists have assumed a relatively simple connection between the theoretical and the practical, an assumption which has sanctioned the quest for a 'correct' theoretical perspective, this being seen as the guarantor of an effective politics. In the following chapters we shall suggest that this view of the connection between theory and practice and the concept of 'reductionism' which it sanctions is problematic.

5

Contemporary debates on the capitalist state

Given the enormous output of Marxist literature on the state during the last fifteen years it is obviously impossible to refer to more than a small amount of it in a single chapter. Our intention here, therefore, is to isolate three major variations of state theory. Though these three approaches exhibit very real differences they also reproduce common theoretical problems, some of these being contemporary versions of those which arise in classical Marxist state theory.

Poulantzas's theory of the state

Poulantzas's stated aim is to establish a theory of the political level of the complex totality that comprises the social formation. Simultaneously, this exercise is an intervention in practical socialist politics and in theory, the concepts which emerge from this theory, notably that of 'power bloc', being 'concepts of strategy' (Poulantzas, 1975, p. 24). He shares with state derivation theory – at least until his later work – the view that the state is fundamentally a capitalist state and that it cannot be the objective of an effective reformist politics, as social democrats, or 'right-Eurocommunist' proponents of the 'state monopoly capitalist' thesis have argued. This view is justified by the claim that the state is an 'expression' of class contradictions and powers (Poulantzas, 1975, p. 164; see also 1976, p. 71 and 1978, pp. 129–132. This relationship of 'expression' is represented in a variety of ways in Poulantzas's work, among which one finds 'condensation', 'crystallization', 'concentration' and 'materialization'). The state has no power of its own and is therefore rigorously class reducible: 'by state power one can only mean the power of certain classes to whose interests the state corresponds' (Poulantzas, 1976, p. 73). Since it lacks power of its own, the reformist view that the state can be won for socialism is said to be an illusion, there being nothing to 'win'. In accordance with this, Poulantzas, like the state derivationists, concludes that 'class struggle', rather than 'reformism', has to be placed at the top of the socialist political agenda.

The state is an expression of class conflicts and contradictions on two fronts; those within the bourgeoisie and those between the bourgeoisie and the working class. In this respect, the forms assumed by the capitalist state depend upon 'the precise relations between the dominant classes and fractions which are themselves the effects of the principal contradictions between the bourgeoisie and the working class' (Poulantzas, 1975, p. 98). Poulantzas, however, pays particular attention to the former conflicts, considering the manner in which the state expresses contradictions within the bourgeois 'power bloc', the latter signifying a phenomenon which is peculiar to capitalist formations and whose emergence is said to be indicated in Marx's analysis of the plurality of dominant classes and fractions in mid-nineteenth century France.

Despite the fact that the capitalist state is a product of contradictions within the bourgeoisie, it is claimed that it condenses such contradictions into a 'specific internal unity' (Poulantzas, 1972, p. 247) which enables it to carry out the function of providing order within the social formation. This justifies Poulantzas's view that the state is 'the factor of cohesion of a social formation and the factor of reproduction of the conditions of production' (1972, p. 246). Such cohesion is established by the state's organization and representation of the interests of the 'hegemonic fraction' within the power bloc. In the current phase of capitalism, the hegemonic fraction is monopoly capital, the state comprising the political unifier and organizer of monopoly capitalist hegemony within the bourgeoisie.

Although the state primarily represents the interests of this fraction it enjoys a 'relative autonomy' with respect to it and other classes and fractions. This does not mean that the state's autonomy derives from its institutional form. 'Relative autonomy', in Poulantzas's sense, is a class-based concept which 'stems from . . . the contradictory relations of power between the different social classes' (1976, p. 71). Moreover, the state is not here conceived as relatively autonomous from capital, but from specific fractions of capital.

Consequently, it is claimed that the state is not a 'thing', but a 'condensation of a balance of forces' (Poulantzas, 1975, p. 98). Because state policies take account of the need for cohesion of the power bloc, non-hegemonic classes and fractions can find political expression in certain 'pertinent effects'. The state's autonomy is therefore manifested in the policies and measures 'that each of these classes and fractions, through its specific presence in the state and the resulting play of contradictions, manages to have integrated into state policy' (Poulantzas, 1978, p. 135).

The state, then, overwhelmingly serves the interests of the hegemonic class or fraction, but its 'specific internal unity' guarantees that the dominant class remains the bourgeoisie as a whole. The state ultimately expresses the class powers and interests of the entire bourgeoisie, but the relative autonomy it enjoys prevents it, in Poulantzas's view, from constituting a simple 'tool' of capital. On the one hand, it is not the mere instrument of the fraction which dominates. On the other hand, its unity enables it to serve the *general* interests of capital in the long term. Indeed, such unity gives it an effectivity as organizer of the dominant class, so that it is involved in 'formulating and openly expressing the tactics required to produce its power' (Poulantzas, 1978, p. 32).

The view of the state as an expression of class powers is intended to provide a corrective to those theories which see it as either an 'instrument' without autonomy, or a 'neutral subject' with total autonomy. According to Poulantzas, the common problem with both positions is that they conceive the relationship of state and classes as one of externality, where one subdues the other. It is precisely this conception of 'externality' that Poulantzas rejects in claiming that the state 'expresses' class relations (1978, p. 131).

Now this denial of the 'externality of the state' vis-à-vis capital raises problems for the type of discourse which Poulantzas wants to construct, for it calls into question the very 'specificity' of the state/politics 'level' which his work is intended to theorize. In other words, if one wants to theorize the state as a specific and irreducible 'level' of the (complex) social totality, as Poulantzas does, the denial of its 'externality' from capital amounts to something of a contradiction. For if the state merely 'expresses' class powers and has no externality, one denies its constitution as an agent, distinct from capital, which can bear a relation to it. The problem is, in effect, a variation of that found in classical Marxism where the state is conceived simultaneously as an expression of class powers and a condition of their being.

In Poulantzas's later work, it might seem that he recognizes the nature of this problem since, for the first time, he pays explicit attention to the 'institutional' aspects of the state, any consideration of which he had previously rejected as 'structuralist'. In this later version the state is considered to be

> a specialized and centralized apparatus of a peculiarly political nature, comprising an assemblage of impersonal, anonymous functions whose form is distinct from that of economic power; their ordering rests on the axiomatic force of law-rules distributing the spheres of activity or competence and on a legitimacy derived from the people-nation. In the modern state all these elements are incorporated in the organization of its apparatuses. (Poulantzas, 1978, p. 54)

Here the state is seen to have a specifically political membership, a capacity for delegation, hierarchies of competence; it is given legal and cultural recognition and legitimation and so on. In short, it might appear that the state is a specific social agent, set apart from capital in a relation of 'externality', which enables it to perform certain necessary functions towards the maintenance of capitalist relations of production. Poulantzas, it would appear, is obliged to recognize the state's institutional structure.

In some respects this recognition is a real one for the perspective which it implies sanctions Poulantzas's eventual adoption of a 'left-Eurocommunist' political position. What is less convincing, however, is his ability to sustain that recognition in a rigorous theoretical sense. At this level, the recognition is something of a grudging one. In *State, Power, Socialism*, for example, he appears to present a quite different conception of state power from that outlined previously when he suggests that state apparatuses 'are no mere appendages of power, but play a role in its constitution'. But, seeming to fear the theoretical implications of this suggestion, he immediately qualifies it:

> in the relationship between power and apparatuses . . . the fundamental role is played by the class struggle, whose field is none other than that of relations of power . . . struggles always have primacy over . . . apparatuses or institutions . . . the state is . . . a *site* and a centre of the exercise of power, but it possesses no power of its own. (Poulantzas, 1978, pp. 45 and 148)

This replicates the position Poulantzas had argued for the previous decade, a view based upon the primacy of class relations and 'economic determination in the last instance'. This position reproduces the classic contradiction; the state is only 'fundamentally capitalist' because it is economically reducible; yet its effects produce conditions necessary to capitalism and thereby ensure its irreducibility.

Like Marx and Engels, then, Poulantzas tries to combine two incompatible forms of determination. One cannot explain these theoretical contradictions away by invoking Poulantzas's conversion to 'left-Eurocommunism' as 'proof' of his final break with all forms of reductionist theory. Nor can one eliminate the most problematic elements from his discourse by calling them 'structuralist residues' (Jessop, 1982, p. 191). For such strategies are unable to recognize Poulantzas's failure to conceive institutions and apparatuses as potential conditions of existence and 'means' of the 'class struggle' of which he speaks. Instead, we are presented with a conception of struggle which is seemingly conditionless. This theoretical failing is compounded by his attempts to identify the state both as an expression of class relations and as a 'strategic field' (Poulantzas, 1978, p. 138). Commendable as this project might be Poulantzas's analysis renders it impossible. For having conceived the state as an expression of class relations, and having denied the 'externality' of the state to those relations, he is left without a theoretical criterion for demarcating the state as a 'strategic field'. There is in consequence a necessary 'slippage' whereby anything which is alleged to reproduce class relations is conceived as part of the state apparatus. Poulantzas leaves us with the impression that the state is simply everything and everywhere. It is, indeed, significant that although he adopts Althusser's distinction between 'ideological' and 'repressive' state apparatuses with certain reservations, Poulantzas considers that the greatest merit of that distinction lies in its 'politicization' of all social relations (1978, p. 34). But whatever merit this might have for confronting discourses which Poulantzas would regard as 'bourgeois ideology', it is heavily outweighed by the strategic emptiness of a view of state apparatuses as ubiquitous. Poulantzas is left with an insurmountable problem. Whether one ascribes to him his 'early' project of 'smashing' the state apparatus, or his 'later' one of transforming it from within and without, it is impossible to isolate the 'strategic field' to be confronted.

Indeed, this analysis leaves us with the uncomfortable inference that study of state institutions is something of an irrelevance. This is an inevitable consequence of the attempt to argue that the state exhibits both a 'relative autonomy' and a 'specific internal unity' (Poulantzas, 1973b, pp. 255ff., 264, 288−9, and 1978, pp. 131−3). The postulate of 'unity' is necessary, in Poulantzas's view, to counter those 'pluralistic' images of the state which see it as a set of institutions to be 'parcelled out'. But he recognizes that such a postulate casts doubt on the 'relative autonomy' of the state. His solution is to regard the state as a unity under the dominance of a 'power bloc'.

The effect of this view, an effect which appears time and time again in positions which adopt the materialist conception of politics, is that 'politics' appears at two levels in the analysis. What one might call 'politics proper' is considered to be constituted by class relations and conflicts − in particular those within the power bloc. 'Politics', in its institutional guise, is a reflection or expression of this. In other words the state is effectively a void which 'represents the political unity of this bloc' (Poulantzas, 1976, p. 73).

But this destroys much of the rationale for studying the state. The functions which the state is said to perform for capital (organization and cohesion) are, by implication, superfluous. The political unity of the power bloc is already guaranteed prior to the state being called upon, by the mere existence of capital under the dominance of its hegemonic fraction. For however fractionalized it might appear, the unity of capital is reflected in the unified state apparatus. As Poulantzas says; 'the capitalist state always expresses a specific internal unity, the unity of the power of hegemonic class or fraction' (1973a, p. 48). The bourgeoisie already possesses a unitary set of political interests and powers, and a capacity for realizing them. One is left with the disturbing conclusion that capital, being represented by the concept of power bloc as a super-ficially fragmented political unity, has the capacity to secure its own conditions of existence. Poulantzas's claim to examine the state as a 'strategic field', and his later emphasis on analysing the 'materiality' of the state apparatus, is therefore difficult to take seriously. The central concepts of Poulantzian state analysis (power bloc, hegemony and the unity of classes and the state) make any genuine analysis of state apparatuses impossible.

State derivation theory

Altvater provides one of the earlier contributions to the German 'state derivation' debate and it is the approach presented in that contribution which offers a good example of the so-called 'capital—logic' perspective. Here the necessity for a 'separate' state is derived from the relation between capitals. Altvater maintains that under the CMP capital is unable to produce, through the acts of individual capital units, the preconditions of capital accumulation which constitute its social conditions of existence. A separate institution, not subject to the limits of capital, is therefore required. This institution develops in the form of the state as 'a specific form expressing the general interests of capital' (Altvater, 1973, p. 99), a view similar to Engels's conception of it as an 'ideal personification of the total national capital'.

The state serves, then, to provide infrastructure, to maintain a legal system appropriate to capitalism and so on, functions which individual capital units cannot perform because of the effects of laws of competition. Altvater suggests that capital, left to itself, destroys its own social foundation (wage labour, the environment etc.), the state, according to this view, serving to uphold the long term interests of 'capital in general' against the short term interests of individual capitalists.

It should be obvious that Altvater's position has precisely the same shortcomings as Poulantzas's. In the first place we are again confronted with a conception of the state as 'expression' of capital's interests and all its attendant problems. Secondly, Altvater, like Poulantzas, has to conceive the state in a very restricted sense. Indeed, Altvater's view of it is doubly restricted by the functionalism which is implicit in his discourse. State apparatuses and institutions do not, then, constitute means of production of policies, but are mere filters through which the logic of capital is translated into legislation. Like Poulantzas, Altvater assumes that the powers, capacities and fundamental interests of capital exist independently of any determinate conditions of production. Rather than posing the 'interests of capital' as a problem for analysis, both authors seek to homogenize the potentially diverse field of interests into unified totalities. Towards this end the concept 'capital in general' (Altvater) and 'power bloc' serve exactly the same function.

Moreover, it is by no means clear that 'capital—logic' is even able to 'establish that the capitalist state is an essential element in the social reproduction of capital' (Jessop, 1977, p. 363). Capital in general is said to logically dictate through its laws of motion that certain functions will be performed. But this tells us precisely nothing about the institutional forms which, it is alleged, will perform these functions. And again, if the political content of state activity is defined outside the apparatuses of politics, whether by the logic of capital, or by the structure of class relations within the power bloc, the very relevance of state analysis is called into question.

Many proponents of state derivation theory take the view that 'capital—logic' provides a less fruitful basis for analysis than the various types of 'class—historical' approaches. Hirsch, for example, rejects the logical-functional approach of Altvater, arguing instead that one cannot discuss the actions and functions of the state until its historic form has been defined. In his view, the bourgeois state is 'the expression of a specific historical form of class rule and not simply . . . the bearer of particular social functions' (Hirsch, 1978, p. 63). The state arises, then, not from the logic of capital, but from class conflicts and 'political movements and interests' (Hirsch, 1978, p. 65).

Hirsch insists that state theory is to be founded upon 'accumulation and crisis', central to which is the concept of the 'tendency of the rate of profit to fall' (TRPF). Since TRPF features constant class struggle, accumulation will, it is said, lead to more and more overt class conflict. Capitalist 'collapse' is prevented only by the production of 'counter tendencies' (see Marx, 1864) and their successful mobilization by capitalists.

What Hirsch has in mind here is a theory of capitalist development which sees general tendential laws 'mediated' by empirical and historical conditions. The state cannot be deduced from abstract laws, but is a product of the mediation of such laws by 'concrete political processes' (Hirsch, 1978, p. 82).

In the view of many, Hirsch's approach provides a corrective to Altvater's functionalism, notably in its capacity to question the thing which Altvater takes for granted — the state's ability to fulfil its functions. Both Gerstenberger (1976) and Holloway and Picciotto (1978) suggest that Hirsch's work is novel because it calls into question the state's capacity to act adequately for capital in general.

Though Hirsch avoids 'capital—logic's' crude functionalism, his work exhibits serious ambiguities and contradictions. In the first place, he fails to resolve the problem of the relationship of 'logic' and 'history' or 'form' and 'content', contrary to what he and others claim. All that we are presented with is a view of the structure of the CMP as 'mediated' by class conflicts and political struggles. This produces a theoretical conclusion which is mere banality when Hirsch insists that state theory has to address not only the law of value and its effects, but 'the whole of the social, political and national conditions of the production of the social formation' (1978, p. 82). After all, the realization that state theory demands an analysis of social and political conditions is hardly a monumental advance, especially if the relationship between those conditions and the CMP remains untheorized.

Hirsch's analysis also fails *because* of the 'class—historical' approach which is meant to provide a salvation from functionalism and reductionism. There is, in fact, a particular form of 'reductionism' at work here, for Hirsch assumes that the empirical conditions which 'mediate' the structural constraints of the CMP are class-based. By making this reduction Hirsch necessarily determines the character of political and social practices and the range of their possible outcomes. Political practices by the state, or for that matter, those directed at the state, are, therefore, doubly structured by (a) the structure of relations in the CMP and (b) the structure of interests which constitute classes as contradictory political forces. Hirsch's advance over Altvater is, then, illusory. There are no specific limitations or possibilities in state action as politics is a dialogue between two forces. Either capitalist relations will be reproduced (Altvater) or they may not (Hirsch). But nothing much of any substance can be said about conditions and situations that exist within and between these extremes. The final irony is that when Hirsch confronts substantive political issues he is forced to amend this class reductionism and recognize the state as an entity in its own right with 'bureaucracies, governing cliques, party apparatuses and bureaucratic mass organizations' (1978, p. 107). For this recognition, his British sympathizers, Holloway and Picciotto, accuse him of lapsing into Poulantzian 'politicism'.

Holloway and Picciotto's refined version of the 'class—historical' approach has had considerable influence in British Marxist circles in recent years, the authors considering that their position resolves some of the 'politicist' problems in Hirsch's analysis which so offend their own materialist sensibilities. Two aspects of their work are relevant to the present discussion. First, they claim that they resolve the 'dualism' which dominates Marxism — notably the problem of the relative weight which is to be granted to 'base' vis-à-vis 'superstructure'. Secondly, and to their credit, they make a much more deliberate attempt than the German writers to outline some of the strategic implications of the state derivation approach.

Like Hirsch, they maintain that state analysis must depend upon an examination of the relationship between 'capital accumulation' and 'class struggle' (Holloway and Picciotto, 1977, p. 76; 1978, p. 1). Capital accumulation is here understood to have two aspects. Firstly, it is a process beset by the inherent contradictions of capitalist laws of motion.

Secondly, it is not to be equated with 'economics' as a sphere set apart from 'political' class struggle. Holloway and Picciotto reject the view that the social formation comprises discrete 'levels' of 'economics', 'politics' and 'ideology', claiming that a truly materialist state theory will mirror Marx's critique of political economy. It is argued, then, that the state is manifested as a 'fantastic form' or 'thing' which conceals (as 'appearance') its essential constitution as a social relation, just as the 'commodity form' obscures social relations of production. It follows from this that the analysis supplants the conventional problem of the relationship of the 'economic' (base) and the 'political' (superstructure) to ask instead: 'what is it about relations of production under capitalism that makes them assume separate economic and political forms?' (Holloway and Picciotto, 1977, p. 78).

The state, then, is conceived not as a 'level' of the social formation, but as a form of appearance of the 'capital relation'. There is, in effect, a quite different conception of social totality at work here. The social formation is not seen as a unity of constituent levels 'structured in dominance'. Instead it is constituted by the 'capital relation'. The state, then, is not a 'relatively autonomous' level of the social formation, but a 'fetishized form' of the capital relation. The view of the capitalist totality as a 'structure in dominance' gives way to a conception of it as 'unity in separation' (Holloway and Picciotto, 1976, p. 6).

The problem of the relationship between the separate 'levels' of the totality is, therefore, supplanted by the view that the totality is already and always a unity, but one which gives the illusion of separation. The significance of this should be apparent. By refusing to give a special existence to politics, ideology, law, etc., one does not have to face the problem which has dogged generations of Marxists of having to posit relations of determinacy between them and the economy (see especially Picciotto, 1979). In short, one avoids the problem of assigning relative weight to 'structure' over 'conjuncture', 'logic' over 'history' and 'base' over 'superstructure' by fusing such dualisms into the 'capital relation' as constitutive totality.

It is with this end in mind that Holloway and Picciotto claim that it is a mistake to draw a distinction between 'form' (logical) analysis and 'historical' analysis. Instead they maintain that Marx's categories are always and already 'simultaneously logical and historical categories' (Holloway and Picciotto, 1978, p. 27). It is for this reason that class struggle in its specific historical form is considered to be the constitutive element of the capital relation. In this view, it is the essence of the 'logical' and lawful structure of capitalism as well as the agency of political struggle. As such, it functions to bridge the sides of the traditional dichotomy. For this reason the concept of TRPF is placed at the centre of state analysis, since it is considered to epitomize the fusion of 'logic' and 'history', the laws of motion which give rise to it also producing the 'counter tendencies' which comprise the political process of 'restructuring'.

If the analysis produced avoids Hirsch's 'politicism', it is only by the adoption of a relatively rigid 'economism', for despite their emphatic denial of the polarization of logic and history and their refusal to posit causal relations between them, they insist that the restructuring process is a product of 'form determined class struggle' (Holloway and Picciotto, 1977, p. 92). Indeed, class struggle is 'bounded by the exigencies of accumulation' to such an extent that the 'political conditions' which affect restructuring are simply 'left aside for the sake of exposition' as 'myriad extraneous circumstances which affect the way in which the crisis presents itself' (Holloway and Picciotto, 1977, p. 93).

Moreover, the attempt to avoid the problem of positing causal relations between 'levels' of the social formation by re-thinking the concept of unity merely reproduces the traditional dichotomy in a new way. The 'capital relation' is an essence with causal priority. Politics and ideology are forms of appearance, or effects without effect. Ultimately, Holloway and Picciotto re-enter the terrain of theoretical haggling over causality, 'relative autonomy' merely being supplanted by an indeterminate conception of causality which is 'form determined' yet 'dialectical'.

If this conception of social totality is ultimately as incoherent as that of the Althusserians, the effects of that incoherence are seen most clearly in their attempts to theorize that totality in class terms and apply such a view to the strategic context. The concepts of class and class struggle are particularly central to this view of political strategy, a strategy which again has its basis in the theory of fetishism.

The conjunction of the theory of fetishism with an emphasis on class struggles in strategic discussion is by no means accidental. Chapter 3 has already shown how Marxism views economic and social relations as 'personifications' of class relations. According to this view, classes are the effective agents of social relations, capitalist 'forms' of politics being reproduced by categories of agents having the capacity to 'personify' form determined functions. This view depends, to a large extent, upon the concept of 'fetishism', that being the process whereby empty subjects are endowed with the necessary capacities to recognize and misrecognize the structure of social relations and in so doing, reproduce the capitalist totality of forms.

Holloway and Picciotto's merit lies in their attempt to outline the strategic implications of such a conception. That strategy begins again from the concept of 'form', it being argued that since historical materialism is a 'science of forms' (Holloway, 1979, p. 7), socialist strategy must be the product of such a science. Considered in this light, then, the state may be regarded as an apparatus which serves to reproduce social relations as 'things', achieving this end by literally 'fragmenting class relations' and reproducing them in non-class 'forms'. By way of example, it might be argued that the welfare state confronts problems of poverty and deprivation by denying their relationship to class exploitation and domination, in order to process them as 'individual issues' (Holloway, 1979, p. 18ff.). The socialist strategic response to such a situation places a new meaning on the concept of 'socialist transformation'. The task for socialist political activists is

> not to work through bourgeois forms to gain positions of 'power' and 'influence' . . . but to work against these forms, to develop through practice, material forms [sic] of counter organization which express and consolidate the underlying unity of the resistance to class oppression. (Holloway, 1979, p. 28)

The socialist solution is to mobilize a variety of organizations (unions, shop steward committees, anti-racist organizations; women's groups, campaigns against expenditure cuts, etc.) around a strategy which raises the 'real' issues of class domination and oppression. In short, the strategy is one of 'total class struggle' (Holloway and Picciotto, 1976, p. 4; 1977, p. 80).

There are, however, serious problems with this view of politics. Again we have a conception of the state apparatus as an expression of something else — this time of the development of social relations as 'forms'. Despite making attempts to acknowledge the role of state institutions in the politics of 'fragmentation', the reproduction of fetishized social relations seems, in Holloway and Picciotto's view, to have no political conditions of existence. Despite rather tenuous attempts to recognize the state as an 'apparatus', rather than just a 'form' (Holloway, 1979, p. 25), essentially the state is only a 'form process', an expression of the manner in which the capital relation develops and manifests itself.

This view of politics leaves the authors with another serious problem. How is one to evaluate those 'forms' of left-wing politics which are not 'true' socialism — that is, types based on strategies other than 'total class struggle', which do not reject the state form *in toto*? On this, the authors are, to say the least, ambivalent. They are loathe to reject forms of politics such as unionism, or social democratic 'reformism' out of hand, arguing that their purpose is not to 'belittle the importance of such struggle but to underline its essential limitations' (Holloway and Picciotto, 1976, p. 6). Yet there is a problem here with regard to the *calculation* of such limitations, for given their theoretical position, all one can say is that 'reformism' and unionism are not socialism proper and imply a blanket rejection of them. Despite protestations to the contrary, this much is suggested in their view of the Factory Acts and the postwar welfare reforms: 'Class struggle (within bourgeois forms) merely acts as mediating factor in the establishment of the interests of capital in general' (Holloway and Picciotto, 1976, p. 6). What this implies is that anything which is not socialist politics proper has to be bourgeois politics, a theme within Marxism which we shall explore more fully later.

It is clear that Holloway and Picciotto, in common with other positions previously discussed, adopt a view of political practice as fundamentally conditionless. The state thus 'fragments' (cf. Poulantzas's 'disorganizes') an already constituted working class unity which is a concomitant of capitalist relations of production. Given this view, socialism simply amounts to the production of counter organizations which 'express' such underlying unity and in this respect are no less ineffectual (as merely efficient expressions of some allegedly underlying working class unity) than the state is (as an expression of 'form determined' processes). The call for a 'total class struggle', whatever its propagandist virtues, amounts, then, to a peculiarly limited mode of socialist politics.

Finally, what are we to make of the call for a politics of 'transformation' by class struggle? Clearly, this strategy rests upon the possibility of carrying out socialist politics *outside* 'bourgeois forms'. But two things have to be considered here. First, this assumes the existence of a 'real' and unconditional politics 'outside' political organizations and institutions, a view similar to that adopted by Poulantzas. But, if state theory is to have any justification at all, its purpose must be to identify state apparatuses as potential sites of socialist political practice. The state is not a 'form', but provides conditions of existence of capitalist relations through the effectivity which resides in its apparatuses. In this respect, it is an inevitable terrain of socialist intervention and one which is by no means inherently limited. Whatever specific limitations such 'form' directed politics might have are defined not by reference to the self-reproducing structure of the capital relation, but by a consideration of political objectives, forms of organization and conditions.

Secondly, the call for an abandonment of the sphere of 'bourgeois' politics for truly 'proletarian' forms of organization is vacuous. However justified the view that new forms of political organization may be required for an effective socialist politics, such forms are necessarily implicated in existing political relations. As such, they are subject to the effects of practices by state apparatuses and organizations. 'Proletarian' forms of organization will be subject, for example, to 'bourgeois' legal relations unless they are terrorist organizations and to 'bourgeois' economic relations once they undertake financial activities. Whether socialists like it or not such 'fetishized' relations are the political terrain under which they are obliged to operate in capitalist societies and no amount of 'fetishizing' them will make them go away.

Towards neo-Gramscian analysis

Gramsci's analysis of politics and the state, outlined in Chapter 4, raises three important issues. First, it is presented as a challenge to 'economism' and, indeed, to all vulgar 'base' *versus* 'superstructure' conceptions of politics. Not surprisingly, then, it is considered by many Marxists to provide a genuine alternative to reductive conceptions of political power. Secondly, the expanded definition of the state is intended, both as a resolution of certain theoretical problems and as means of widening the potential scope of socialist political intervention vis-à-vis the state. Thirdly, the concept of hegemony is, amongst other things, a way of defining socialist transformation as a revolutionary 'process' occurring within the context of 'bourgeois' social relations.

These three matters are crucial to an understanding of how neo-Gramscian analysis develops. They are particularly significant in that they raise two areas for consideration, both of which have provided a basis for recent work by writers who adopt this perspective. First, they open up the question of the relationship between the power of classes and the power of other entities. The problem of class power/non-class power is, however, only part of a more general question which arises in neo-Gramscian analysis, namely, what is the relationship of class agency to non-class agency? Secondly, they pose the problem of the state in much more of a 'strategic' sense than is evident in various other schools of Marxism, for the concept of hegemony is concerned primarily with problems of socialist political calculation in the context of the 'integral' state.

These observations, together with others — Gramsci's attempt to produce a non-teleological theory for example — make it easy to understand the so-called 'Gramsci boom'. For the suggestion that 'hegemony' constitutes a field of struggle, and the consequent implication that the reproduction of capitalist relations may be problematic, has offered a basis for the study of 'crisis' in state forms and political regimes. This has obviously been appealing to Marxists working in the context of capitalist recession.

Our intention in what remains of this chapter will be to provide a backcloth to some aspects of neo-Gramscian analysis, a task which we shall pursue by addressing some general critical comments to certain Gramscian themes. Consideration of the work of some neo-Gramscian writers will be held over until we examine some of the problems of class analysis and socialist political calculation in the following chapters. This approach is justified, we would maintain, because the most important aspects of neo-Gramscian work concern the complex problem of the relationship of class/non-class relations.

Let us begin by considering the object 'the state'. There is hardly much doubt that Gramsci failed to define 'the state' and 'civil society' consistently (see Nowell Smith and Hoare in Gramsci, 1971, p. 207). Jessop tries to resolve this problem by maintaining that Gramsci is important, not for his definition of the state, but for his analysis of state power, a conception which allows him to look at the problem of the state from the perspective of 'the totality of social relations in a given society' (1982, pp. 146–7). Jessop rightly suggests that this enables Gramsci to give primacy to 'class struggle' over the institutional structure of the state, a position later adopted by Poulantzas.

Three problems arise here. First, if class struggle is given primacy over state institutions, how does one recognize the effects of those institutions? We return, again, to the classical dilemma of state as 'expression' or 'means' of power. Secondly, at the theoretical level, what justifies social relations being homogenized into a 'totality' whose political unity is symbolized in the concept of 'integral state'. Or, to put it another way, why are the various sites of power and conflict in 'political' and 'civil' society conceived as elements of 'the state' in its integral form? Thirdly, at the strategic level, is the concept of integral state the boon it is alleged to be by Gramscian writers? Though it may, indeed, provide a basis for a broader conception of socialist politics, we have already seen the danger of conceiving all social relations as part of the state. For if social relations constitute a totality, and that totality is symbolized in the integral state, how does one gauge the particular importance of interventions in specific areas of that totality?

Gramsci's definition of the state relates to the wider problem of base and superstructure. Indeed his work may be seen as a partial attempt to transform the terms of that distinction. He is, for example, aware of the difficulty of drawing a rigorous distinction between the two sides, in one instance citing the case of the printing industry which is both an object of property and class division ('base') and an element of the production of ideology ('superstructure'). Though this recognition is never systematically worked out it provides the basis for an emphasis on the materiality of ideology, a perspective developed more fully by Althusser.

In principle Gramsci's recognition has great potential. For one thing, a dissolution of the base/superstructure dichotomy would enable Marxists to avoid much of the haggling over 'relative determination' which has dominated theoretical debate, some of the consequences of which we shall observe in the following two chapters. For another, it offers a potential means of dispensing with what frequently appear to be artificial divisions between 'the economic', 'the political' and 'the ideological' dimensions of social relations. However, some of this potential is lost by Gramsci's insistence on retaining a 'totalizing' principle for analysing social relations. Gramsci, like some of his neo-Gramscian followers (e.g.,

Urry, 1981), adopts a view which deconstructs the base/superstructure distinction, thereby removing the attendant problem of the relationship between elements, only to reconstruct it as part of an 'ensemble of social relations'. Once the ensemble is invoked, however, one has to find a general principle of determination which binds the elements of the totality into an 'ensemblement'. In the case of Gramsci, this is, ultimately, the function of the concept of hegemony. The point may be illustrated by considering Gramsci's approach to teleology.

It is clear that one of Gramsci's intentions is to construct a non-teleological theory of politics and the social formation. This objective is seen by some contemporary writers as a fundamental strength of the Gramscian position. Laclau, for example, regards that position as a corrective to the errors of economism, Gramsci avoiding 'all temptation to conceive society as an ensemble unified by abstract articulations *prior* to the historical forms which assume hegemonic practices' (1980b, p. 255). According to this view, the economy does not constitute the essence of an abstract logic which directs social relations along some pre-determined course, or structures it as a social unity: 'the type of unity existing in a social formation does not depend on essential and necessary articulations but on concrete social articulations' (Laclau, 1980b, p. 254).

Gramsci's basis for theorizing such 'social articulations' is clearly to be found in the concept of hegemony, a concept which sanctions a view of the unity of the social formation being historically and politically constructed, rather than economically and logically structured:

> For Gramsci, history and society are no longer the space in which an abstract logic reduces conjunctural and political specificity to a purely empirical and contingent moment, since society possesses no unity other than that furnished by the political articulations which, at various levels, result from the relation between antagonistic social forces. (Laclau and Mouffe, 1981, p. 20)

How then, we might ask, does Gramsci conceive those 'antagonistic social forces' which disrupt or construct the unity of the social formation? In particular, how does he conceive the relationship of classes and non-class forces to the process of hegemony? For it is obvious that Gramsci, in seeking to construct a theory of politics and ideology which avoids class reductionism, is obliged to recognize the 'specificity' of non-class forces vis-à-vis classes.

It is by no means apparent, however, that Gramsci succeeds in doing this. For one thing, there is an obvious imprecision in his various references to 'classes', 'masses', 'workers', 'allies' and the like. More serious than this, however, is Gramsci's retention — and it is certainly more than a residue or an aberration contained in his work — of class as a fundamental constituent of the politics of hegemony. For not only does Gramsci conceive hegemony as a relationship between classes, he also retains a conception of fundamental class interests, enabling him to re-insert the diverse ideologies that comprise the field of hegemonic struggle into class-specific terms. In the case of socialist politics then, the hegemonic project Gramsci perceives is one where the Party has to represent the interests of 'popular' (non-class) elements, in order for its own universal and fundamental interests to be finally realized. In this sense, only a fundamental class can be hegemonic (see Mouffe, 1979, p. 183). Gramsci succeeds, then, in avoiding the attribution of a necessary class-belonging to all ideological elements in the short term, but produces a complex class essentialism in the long term. In Chapter 7 we will consider how far neo-Gramscian theorists have been able to cope with this type of problem. For present purposes however, it should be clear that Gramsci's attribution of primacy to class relations over and above non-class elements imposes restrictions on the attempt to produce a discourse which is non-teleological. In particular, it leaves him with a conception of the social formation which, far from having its unity produced by relations between determinate social forces, is structured according to the underlying interests of classes.

This chapter and the previous one have suggested that there is a basic incoherence in the materialist conception of politics and in the various versions of it that comprise Marxist state theory. The ontological and teleological assumptions of the materialist conception come into conflict with Marxism's attempts to recognize the effectivity of specific political conditions. All of the attempts to remedy this problem which have been discussed here lapse into incoherence, inconsistency and ambiguity.

Theoretical incoherence apart, the substantive effects of materialist propositions parallel those discussed in Chapter 3. Whereas in that case their adoption gave rise to the continued failure to examine the effects of legal relations upon the spheres of possession/separation and direction, in the case of the state there is a persistent refusal to grant effectivity to political organizations and institutions. The state, like the capitalist, more often than not becomes a mere 'bearer' of processes, the nature of which is determined elsewhere.

Above all else, this chapter has tried to show that despite the massive re-generation of Marxist analysis in the last fifteen years, and in particular, in spite of the vast outpouring of literature on the state, there has been a failure to theorize state apparatuses and institutions as strategic objects. Socialists are no closer to understanding how to perceive and address the 'problem' of the state. Nor does the literature indicate how 'the state' (as a set of apparatuses) is constituted. Least of all are we offered any indication of what relations pertain between specific parts of the state.

These problems cannot be posed by Marxist state theory because that theory is founded upon the assumption that the state is a totality representing a relatively unified capitalist class and confronting a relatively unified class of workers. In several previous chapters, however, we have called into question the legitimacy of the view that classes may be regarded as unconditional unities, and this conception will be subjected to detailed scrutiny in the following chapters. It should be apparent, however, that in the absence of a conception of class unity (or relative class unity), it can no longer be maintained that the state comprises a unified (or relatively unified) structure. State policy does not constitute the unified reflection of the interests of capital. It has definite conditions of production which reside in state institutions and apparatuses and in a variety of bodies and organizations peripheral to the state. Contrary to the view that the state comprises a unity, it is suggested that the unity of state apparatuses and institutions may, indeed, be problematic in certain circumstance and may, in consequence, offer a potentially fruitful terrain for socialist politics.

Class Analysis and Socialist Political Calculation

6

Marxism and the problem of the working class

The following two chapters will subject the Marxist concept of class to serious scrutiny. Though we shall argue that the Marxist project of class analysis generates insurmountable problems, it has to be admitted that many Marxist writers have paid serious attention to resolving problems traditionally associated with the class concept. For example, much concern has been directed to the so-called problem of 'reductionism', the tendency to 'read off' the political, cultural or ideological from an analysis of the economy in general and of economic class relations in particular. In this respect, Marxists have tried to reconcile two views; that an understanding of class structure is a necessary and essential guide to political practice; that such political practice is irreducible to class structure. In general terms, the typical solution to this problem has been to invoke some version of 'relative autonomy', a solution which, we have already seen, generates its own difficulties.

This attempt to reconcile the relative determination of 'structure' with the relative autonomy of 'practice' is seen no more clearly than in the debates on the location of the working class. In the context of the 'materialist conception of politics' it should be obvious why the problem of the 'boundary' of the working class is regarded as a crucial one. For one thing, the identification of this boundary is not merely an abstract exercise. It involves 'political questions of the greatest importance concerning the role of the working class and of alliances in the transition to socialism' (Poulantzas, 1977, p. 113).

According to this view, questions concerning the structure, size and composition of the working class have direct strategic implications for Marxist politics. For example, the problem of the breadth of definition of the working class has, in the view of some, a direct effect on strategies, a broad definition posing the problem of working class unity, a narrow definition, one of alliances (Hunt, 1977, pp. 83–4). In the view of Wright: 'Above all it matters for developing a viable socialist politics how narrow or broad the working class is seen to be and how its relationship to other classes is understood' (1978, pp. 30–1).

That a 'correct' identification of the precise boundary of the working class is crucial to Marxist political debate should be obvious, for in identifying such a class one is attempting to isolate the very core of socialist politics, the social agent whose class interest provides the potential mass base for socialist political organization.

Two issues arise with respect to this conception of political analysis. In the first place, it is obvious that the entire project of 'political class analysis' rests upon a coherent theoretical connection being maintained between two orders of concepts; those associated with the labour theory of value and those associated with the class concept itself. This follows because the 'objective' basis for contradictory class interests is contained in the inherent conflicts alleged to be generated by the structure of the exploitation process. For Marxism, class interests and conflicts are constructed upon the irreconcilable antagonisms that arise in surplus value production. Thus, if the materialist conception of politics is to have theoretical coherence, it must be possible for 'class analysis' to identify classes, both as groups with conflicting political interests *and* as groups occupying different positions in the process of surplus value production. In the particular case of the working class one should, if one is to be consistent with the materialist view of politics, be able to designate it an 'exploited' class in the strictest sense of that word. In Marxism's view it is because one can posit the existence of 'exploited' and 'exploiting' classes that one can theorize the fundamental political ideologies and practices of determinate societies. Without such a connection being consistently maintained between the concepts of 'class' and 'exploitation' much of the explanatory power of the materialist conception of politics disappears, since any consistent basis for an 'objective' concept of 'class interest' is removed. In fact, Marxism has never been able to maintain such a theoretical connection with any coherence — nor has it, in truth, for reasons of political pragmatism, always sought to do so — a fact which is no more clearly indicated than in contemporary debates on the boundary of the working class.

Secondly, the debate on the boundary of the working class raises serious questions regarding the relationship between class analysis and political calculation. In particular, it is necessary to examine Marxism's view of what class analysis is meant to realize in political calculation and whether such expectations are legitimate. Though a considerable amount of work has been produced by Marxists addressing the 'boundary question' (Becker, 1973—4; Nicolaus, 1967; Urry, 1973; Carchedi, 1977) what follows is not an attempt to intervene substantively in that debate. It is much less concerned with an evaluation of the competing arguments than with a discussion of the rationale behind them. Indeed, it will become apparent from what is said that any substantive intervention would serve no purpose, since one of the things suggested here is that the 'problems' posed by that debate, let alone the 'solutions' to it are without any coherent foundation.

Though Marxism defines classes as agents which possess or are separated from possession of the means of production, the debate on the boundary of the working class is concerned with investigating the additional attributes of separated agents of wage labour. The problem, then, concerns whether the possession of certain of these attributes justifies inclusion in or exclusion from the working class. The rationale behind this involves asking whether or not the possession of particular attributes by given categories of wage labour furnishes them with political interests which make them sympathetic towards truly working class forms of political practice.

The entire discussion of the boundary of the working class may be seen in the context of developments in Western class structure and in socio-logical and Marxist responses to such developments. One particular area of debate has concerned the increase in salaried white collar workers throughout Western industrial societies, a common sociological res-ponse to which has been to propose the progressive decomposition of the class structure itself. Marxist discussion of the boundary of the working class has arisen as a response to positions of this type and to claims concerning the reduction of class conflict which is said to accompany such supposed changes in class structure.

In order to consider the rationale behind much of this discussion we shall concentrate on the work of two authors, Poulantzas and Wright. Such selectivity is justified by the general problems and common issues which their works generate.

Poulantzas and Wright

The problem of class determination is especially crucial for Poulantzas, for whom politics is synonymous with class conflict in a literal sense, there being no social groups 'outside' classes which participate in class struggle (1975, p. 201). In his view, it is necessary for the problem of salaried workers to be posed in class terms, rather than in terms of strati-fication. One should recognize the specific class determination of white collared workers and the political consequences of such recognition — that they possess specific class interests distinct from those of the working class. The French Communist Party (PCF) and other communist parties, it is said, by denying the class membership of such employees, ignore this fact. In Poulantzas's opinion, a recognition of the class determination of such groups suggests that they have to be won over by the working class through alliance, but, that because of their specific class interests, they may, at any time, be lost.

Poulantzas insists that classes have to be defined in 'structural' terms. In other words, they are defined principally, but not exclusively, by their place in the production process. The view that a definition based on production relations alone is not sufficient to define classes is supported by the claim that Marx, Lenin and Mao always recognized political and ideological factors in their discussions of class.

Poulantzas's initial definition of the working class derives from economic criteria associated with the labour theory of value and surplus value production. The crucial 'economic' factor which intervenes in the definition of the working class is the concept of 'productive labour', a concept which has been at the centre of much debate. The view that the concept of productive labour is crucial in defining the working class derives from Marxism's need to establish a rigorous connection between Marx's writings on value and exploitation and the concept of class.

Though Marxists would define classes according to determinate relations of production, many, including Poulantzas, regard such relations as, first and foremost, relations of exploitation, this fact providing the basis for a precise definition of working class interests. In view of this, many writers place an analysis of 'exploitation' at the centre of their identification of classes. Thus, for Braverman, 'the discussion [of productive and unproductive labour] is in reality an analysis of the relations of production and ultimately of the class structure of society' (Braverman, 1974, p. 411). Hodges goes even further: 'class is a group defined by its function in an historically definite system of production as a relatum not of social relations of production in general or of property relations in particular but of specific relations of exploitation' (Hodges, 1961, p. 25).

In all such views, the productive labour criterion may be said to provide the basis for a fundamental difference of class interest between the class which produces surplus value (a process quite distinct from the mere 'realization' of it in 'unproductive labour') and that class which appropriates it. However, when an attempt is made to apply this view in actual class analysis, the result is invariably unsatisfactory. Hodges, for example, argues that commercial workers may be excluded from the working class. Being non-productive labourers, they are exploited differently from productive labourers and because of this it may be said that they belong to a different class. In this instance the *form* of exploitation (extraction of surplus labour only) suggests, for the writer, a particular class location. But elsewhere in the same text, the argument is contradicted. When Hodges identifies the 'intermediate class' he suggests that it contains both productive and unproductive labour. In this case the form of exploitation would appear to suggest nothing at all, since certain categories of productive labour such as managers and supervisors are excluded from the working class and placed in an 'intermediate' position.

Poulantzas's structural approach to class determination constitutes a more sophisticated attempt to deal with this type of problem. His initial justification for the view that the production of surplus value is the decisive criterion in the definition of the working class rests upon a particular interpretation of Marx's claim that 'Every productive worker is a wage labourer, but not every wage labourer is a productive worker' (Marx, 1863–6, p. 1041). In Poulantzas's opinion this may be used to justify the argument that all members of the working class are wage earners, but that not all wage earners are members of the working class. Rather, it is only those wage earners who perform productive labour who may be so included and, indeed, some of these may be excluded on the grounds of the intervention of political and ideological criteria in the overall 'structural' determination of class.

Take first the intervention of political factors in such structural determination. Supervisors and lower managers, it is said, are economically exploited by their performance of productive labour, but they also participate in the political domination of the working class. The supervisors' main function in Poulantzas's view is to extract surplus value from the working class and on this basis they have to be excluded from that class. Consequently, they may be assigned to the 'new petty bourgeoisie'. In a similar fashion it may be argued that ideological factors intervene to produce class divisions within productive labour. Engineers and technicians are usually productive labourers, but they are said to dominate the working class ideologically through the mental–manual labour division. Likewise, they may also be placed in the 'new petty bourgeoisie'.

It is not my intention to evaluate Poulantzas's argument in any detail. The position adopted, however, enables him to forestall the more obvious problems that arise in using the productive labour criterion in class determination. For example, if the working class is equated with productive labour, where is one to place those productive labourers whose political position is frequently opposed to manual labour, such as managers, supervisors and the like? Poulantzas seems to offer a theoretical basis for deciding class location, compared with Hodges's classification by fiat.

In fact, Poulantzas's position is no less arbitrary than Hodges's. The term 'structural determination' does not establish any criteria for claiming the primacy of political or ideological factors in any particular circumstance. We are told that in some cases these factors are decisive, though quite why this is so remains somewhat ambiguous. Moreover, Poulantzas fails to give any clear rationale for allocating given relations to the categories of 'the economic', 'the political' or 'the ideological'. Why, to take a case in point, should we consider relations of production between supervisors and other wage labourers 'political' rather than 'economic'? There is, in other words, a fundamental ambiguity running through Poulantzas's text.

But let us return for the moment to the question of productive labour in the context of class interest. Poulantzas, as we have said, regards it as a necessary but insufficient condition of membership of the working class. All members of the working class are productive labourers, but not all productive labourers are members of the working class. In practice, this amounts, in Poulantzas's case, to a definition of the working class based on industrial manual labour, a view which rests upon his equation of productive labour with labour that produces material commodities. In fact, this indicates a site of difficulty in the Marxist definition of the concept of productive labour itself.

Generally, Marx defines productive labour in the CMP as a specific *social* relation of production: 'the notion of productive labour implies not merely a relation between work and useful effect, between labour and product of labour, but also a specific social relation of production' (1867, p. 517). Indeed, more often than not, he is adamant in his rejection of those such as Smith who conceive the productiveness of labour in 'vulgar materialist' terms.

Marx, however, fails to argue this point with consistency. Significantly, a second conception of productive labour emerges in a number of contexts, the clearest statement of this being found in *Theories of Surplus Value* where we are presented with a 'Supplementary Definition of Productive Labour as Labour which is Realized in Material Wealth' (Marx, 1862–3, p. 397). Here it is suggested that there is an historical tendency for productive labour in the CMP to take on a material form. Marx justifies this view by claiming three things:

(i)   That the entire world of commodities, all spheres of material production, are being formally or really subordinated to the CMP.

(ii)   That all labourers engaged in commodity production are wage labourers, the means of production confronting them as capital.

(iii) That productive labour characteristically realizes itself in commodities, in material wealth.

Now some writers (e.g. Rubin, 1972) have claimed this supplementary definition to be entirely consistent with the dominant one, but it is difficult not to recognize the peculiar equation of 'commodity' and 'material wealth' that Marx presents us with. Gough (1972) notes the problem but is content to gloss over it by calling upon a further Marxian criticism of 'vulgar materialism'. In this case, Marx insists that to speak of the commodity as a 'materialization of labour' is not to equate its social mode of existence with its 'corporeal reality'; rather, it is conceived 'as a definite quantity of social labour'. In this sense, 'it may be that the concrete labour whose result it is leaves no trace in it' (Marx, 1862—3, p. 167).

This argument is, however, hardly convincing for in the very passage where Marx tries to illustrate this principle of 'concrete labour whose result leaves no trace in it' (the labour of transport; 1862—3, pp. 399—400), the concept of materialization is used to make a distinction between material production and 'mere' service. The concept of 'material commodity' (and the term can be found as early as page two of the first volume of *Capital*) constitutes, then, a genuine ambiguity in Marx's attempt to define the concept of productive labour with any rigour.

What is perhaps even more serious than this, however, is the fact that despite complex efforts to use the concept of productive labour in class analysis, there is no clear and unambiguous connection between it and the definition of classes. Though Marxists may speak of the working class as a 'productive' class, or 'exploited' class, there is no effective attempt to specify the connections between the two orders of concepts.

Though Marx and Engels never resolve the theoretical question satisfactorily, the inconsistencies that they exhibit do not pose immediate political problems for their work. Thus, the confusion over whether commercial employees are to be regarded as 'middle classes', situated between workers and capitalists (Marx cited in Bottomore and Rubel, 1963, p. 198) or 'commercial proletarians' (Engels's footnote 39(a) to Marx, 1864, p. 301) hardly amounts to a pressing strategic problem. Contemporary Marxists are, however, faced not only with the same theoretical difficulties but with their strategic implications, given the vast expansion of 'unproductive' employment in modern capitalist economies. In this context, even some of those writers who see a need to found a theory of the working class on the concept of 'exploitation' recognize the difficulties that that implies for Marxist politics — a shrinking proletariat for one. It is interesting that Braverman, having put the productive/unproductive labour distinction at the centre of his class theory is ultimately obliged to regard that distinction as merely 'technical': 'the two masses of labour are not otherwise in striking contrast and need not be counterposed to each other' (Braverman, 1974, p. 423).

The implication behind this claim is that *different* forms of production relation (extraction of surplus value/extraction of surplus labour) can generate *common* class interests and it is this same assumption which provides a basis for Wright's analysis of 'contradictory class locations'.

Accordingly, Wright begins by questioning the view that productive labour represents a class interest distinct from unproductive labour. In his view, assuming that 'the fundamental class interest of the proletariat is the destruction of capitalist relations of production and the construction of socialism, then the question becomes whether productive and unproductive workers have a different interest with respect to socialism'

(Wright, 1978, p. 48). Wright suggests that some Marxists claim unproductive labour to have a 'stake' in exploitation since such labour is said to live off surplus value. He suggests, however, that the problem is not whether such divisions of 'immediate interest' exist within the working class, but whether such divisions generate 'different objective interests in socialism'. In his opinion, none of these divisions of immediate economic interest within the working class 'changes the fundamental fact that all workers by virtue of their position within the social relations of production have a basic interest in socialism' (Wright, 1978, p. 39). Contrary to Poulantzas, for whom the differential form of exploitation constitutes the basis for a difference in interests, Wright argues that whatever the form of economic exploitation, the basic fact is that socialism is a pre-requisite for ending it.

Wright also disputes Poulantzas's use of political and ideological criteria in class determination. He rightly calls into question some of the criteria chosen, also objecting to the fact that deviation from any of the structural criteria that define the working class leads to a positive exclusion from membership. In his opinion this has two problematic consequences. First, it goes against Marxist forms of determination, making political and ideological criteria equal in importance to economic ones. Secondly, it makes for a numerically small working class. This is a particularly serious problem for Wright who sees the question of the size of the proletariat as an issue of 'considerable political importance'.

Rather than excluding 'ambiguous' positions within the class structure from the working class, Wright suggests that they should be regarded as 'occupying objectively contradictory locations within class relations' (1978, p. 61). His own analysis is concerned with elucidating such contradictory locations. Class relations under capitalist relations of production are accordingly analysed in terms of three historical processes; control of labour power; control of the physical means of production; control of investments and resources. The two main 'class forces' in capitalist society, bourgeoisie and proletariat, represent polar class positions within each process. Thus, the bourgeoisie control investment, labour power and the means of production and the proletariat do not. The petty bourgeoisie is defined by the possession of the first and last of these capacities within simple commodity production. 'Contradictory locations' exist where these processes do not correspond to the basic forces within capitalist relations of production or to the petty bourgeoisie in simple commodity production. This enables Wright to propose three contradictory locations within class relations. First, managers and supervisors occupy such a location between the bourgeoisie and proletariat. They have varying degrees of control (total, partial, minimal or none at all) of the means of production, investment and labour power. On the basis of a similar argument small employers occupy a contradictory location between bourgeoisie and petty bourgeoisie. Lastly, semi-autonomous employees occupy such a location between petty bourgeoisie and proletariat. One of the immediate consequences of this position is that it produces a proletariat, numerically much larger than that proposed by Poulantzas — something like half of the population of the USA for example. Indeed, in the case of America: 'The total potential class basis for a socialist movement consisting of the working class and those contradictory locations closest to the working class, is thus probably somewhere between sixty per cent and seventy per cent of the population' (Wright, 1978, p. 87).

Poulantzas and Wright have been selected for consideration because of the clear differences between them. However, rather than pursue those particular differences it is the nature of their common purpose which needs to be considered here. In both cases class analysis is intended to provide a rigorous specification of the 'class basis' for socialism. Towards this end, a correct definition of the working class is crucial, though it is also important to investigate the nature of the groups (classes or contradictory locations) which surround the working class. Building socialism depends on finding a means of drawing such groups into alignment with the working class, without ignoring their distinctiveness from that class.

In this respect, two issues are of particular significance. Firstly, there is the question of how 'class interest' is seen to be constituted. Poulantzas tries to provide a rigorously materialistic/objective basis for such interest by linking it with the performance of productive labour. Usually this argument asserts that unproductive labour, whilst having surplus labour appropriated from it, none the less 'lives off' and gains advantages from capitalism's continued exploitation of surplus value. Wright, along with many others, rejects this view, claiming instead that productive and unproductive labour possess a complementarity of interests by virtue of their common exploitation. Supporters of this view often refer to Marx's claim that unproductive labour itself contributes to the expansion of surplus value and is, in this sense, a necessary component of the exploitation process: 'The commercial worker produces no surplus value directly . . . but adds to the capitalist's income by helping him to reduce the cost of realizing surplus value inasmuch as he performs partly unpaid labour' (Marx, 1864, p. 300; some writers, such as Anderson (1974), argue, quite wrongly, that because groups such as commercial workers contribute to the expansion of productive capital they are therefore productive labourers in the Marxian sense).

Judging this claim in conventional Marxian terms, however, it is highly dubious whether one can suggest, as Wright does, that the mere *fact* of exploitation can generate common class interests, irrespective of the nature of the particular *form*. For in the Marxian view it is precisely the form of exploitation which is decisive in revealing the 'hidden basis' of political and ideological structures and practices. Wright's attempt to gloss over this, like Braverman's, has then, to be considered a dubious piece of Marxism.

There remains a far more serious aspect to this question however. Is either solution to the problem of the constitution of class interest to be considered satisfactory? This remains an issue to be examined in full later. Suffice it to say for now that an adequate theory of political interests need not be restricted by the span of assumptions exhibited in Marxist discourses, though this has invariably been the assumption of most literature.

The second issue concerns the relationship which is said to exist between class analysis and political practice. Wright is unequivocal in arguing that 'it is impossible to deduce any political lessons simply from the analysis of class positions' (1978, p. 108). In his view the whole question is much more complicated. The analysis of class structure may indicate possible limits and constraints on forms of political practice by particular agents, but there can be no simple and unproblematic knowledge of political practice from an analysis of class structure.

However, this view hardly fits in with what Wright has already told us about the working class, whose fundamental class interest 'is the destruction of capitalist relations of production and the construction of socialism' (1978, p. 48). Here it would appear that we *can* draw political conclusions from class analysis. Some classes adopt political ideologies that derive from their class location − the working class and socialism. Some classes are, indeed, constituted as (political) class forces adopting practices which follow from such location. After all, that is why it is so important to define the working class − the 'class basis' of socialist politics. That is also why it matters how broadly or narrowly the working class is defined. There is, in fact, no suggestion of class analysis providing us with a means of gauging the limits or possibilities of forms of political practice. Rather, that practice is deduced from class analysis and determination. In other words, it may be admitted that there is complexity somewhere in the class structure, but it is *known* that the working class is fundamentally socialist and that its opposite class 'force', the bourgeoisie, is its natural political adversary.

Wright's position is, in effect, remarkably similar to Poulantzas's. The latter argues that class analysis is basic to political calculation because politics *is* class conflict. Yet, like Wright, he is uncertain about the precise relationship between class analysis and the political conclusions which one can draw from it. On the one hand, political calculation depends on class analysis. The analysis of class structure is the key to the investigation of practices and ideologies. On the other hand, there is a basic distinction between structures and practices and between the structural determination of classes and the political positions they may adopt. This relationship is one of irreducibility (see especially Poulantzas, 1973b, p. 65).

In view of this, it is suggested that a class may take up a political position which does not correspond to its interests as given to it by structural determination. A typical example of such an occurrence would be the labour aristocracy's adoption of a bourgeois class position. Poulantzas is adamant that the adoption of such a position leaves unaltered the fact that the labour aristocracy remains working class. The intended political relevance of this view is made clear when he refers to the problem of white collar and salaried employees. If such 'petty bourgeois' class fractions adopt proletarian positions in any particular circumstance this does not justify designating them part of the working class. They remain petty bourgeois and in consequence their political position vis-à-vis the working class is unstable. In Poulantzas's view, then, it is imperative that Marxism does not abandon the distinction between structural determination and position, opting merely for an analysis of political positions in any conjuncture. To do this would be to throw away the objective basis that class analysis gives to political calculation (Poulantzas, 1975, p. 16).

Now there are two basic problems arising from this argument. In the first place, the recognition of a gap between class determination and political practice immediately calls into question the entire basis of Poulantzas's critique of PCF, about which *Classes in Contemporary Capitalism* is so concerned. Once it is recognized that a class's political position cannot be derived from its class determination, the *raison d'être* of class analysis is called into question. More specifically, as Hirst has pointed out, Poulantzas's criticism of the PCF falls apart. Even if the PCF's class analysis is erroneous, as is claimed, this cannot constitute a critique of its political programme. Moreover, the irreducibility of the political position of classes has to imply that such positions have conditions of existence outside of class determination. Poulantzas has nothing at all to say about the possible conditions which might account for the gap between a class's structural determination and the political position it may adopt in any given circumstance (see Hirst, 1977, p. 132).

Secondly, what are we to make of the argument that class analysis provides us with some objective basis for making political calculations? The nature of this problem is made clear in Poulantzas's discussion of the politics of the new petty bourgeoisie in the final pages of *Classes in Contemporary Capitalism*. He refutes any simple reductionist conception of petty bourgeois political practice when he claims that certain fractions of that class are 'objectively polarized' towards the working class. Such polarization is of political significance, but he insists that 'we must rid ourselves once and for all of the illusions that have often affected the revolutionary movement throughout its history, to the effect that an objective proletarian polarization of class determination must necessarily lead, in time, to a polarization of class positions' (Poulantzas, 1975, p. 334). Apart from the fact that this merely underlines what has been said above — Poulantzas recognizes the non-class conditions of existence of forms of political practice, but has nothing to say about them — there is a more serious problem. The final recognition of the non-congruence of class determination and political position begs the question of what a detailed class analysis of the new petty bourgeoisie has, in fact, told us. When considered in these terms, far from presenting us with an objective basis for political calculation, it is clear that the analysis produces only a strategic impasse. At best, class analysis does direct political calculation; we 'know' that at some 'fundamental' level the working class is socialist. At worst, however, it tells us precisely nothing; the petty bourgeoisie is a distinct class with determinate interests, but even when polarized in one or other direction its politics is unpredictable. Moreover, even in those cases where class analysis does appear to provide us with political knowledge, there remains a loophole — there are, after all, sections of the proletariat such as the labour aristocracy which adopt non-proletarian practices.

Nor can it be claimed that the recognition of the lack of congruence between class determination and practice is meant to provide a space in which we can think through the objective possibility which class analysis allegedly provides us with. Neither Poulantzas nor Wright has any intention of employing class analysis in such a restricted sense and in this they are typical of Marxist writers on class. For, after all, it is the conception of political practices as reducible to the actions of 'class forces' which provides the rationale for the project of class analysis in the first place.

The working class as agent of political practice

So far it has been suggested that Marxists tackling the 'boundary problem' fail to provide a coherent theory of the mechanisms whereby politics is 'more or less representative' of class interests. But what of the assumption that underpins that argument — that classes in general and the working class in particular constitute agents of political practice?

To begin with it is necessary to specify precisely how Marxism considers classes to be social and political agents. For one thing, although Marxism sees politics as 'class conflict', nobody takes this in its literal sense to mean that the political conflicts which arise in Parliament, in the factory, on the streets and so on, are acted out in a physical sense by classes. Instead, as we have seen, it is maintained that the collectivities which occupy the arena of politics represent class interests. Leaving aside the problems that that assumption raises for the moment, it is clear that the concept of 'representation' assumes that there is something identifiable and cohesive enough to *be* represented. In other words, the notion of 'representation of class interests' implies some minimal degree of class cohesion. For classes to be effective agents of political practice it is necessary, then, for them to enjoy some degree of class unity.

At the same time, however, Marxism has been forced to recognize that the relatively unified working class is, in practice, beset by heterogeneity and division. The question arises, then, of the theoretical status that may be given to this heterogeneity. On this, the Marxist answer has been unequivocal:

> Since Bernstein, the opportunists have striven constantly to portray the objective economic stratifications in the proletariat as going so deep and to lay such emphasis on the similarity in the 'life situations' of the various proletarian, semi-proletarian and petty bourgeois strata that in consequence the unity and the autonomy of the class was lost. (Lukacs, 1971, pp. 323−4)

Lukacs' comment serves both as a critique of Weberian attempts to dilute the working class and as a statement of Marxist orthodoxy. For according to the orthodox view, the working class has a fundamental unity and a coherent class interest which makes it a repository of socialist politics. To what extent, then, is Marxism able to reconcile this view with a consideration of the real divisions which cut across working class unity? Let us examine some of the ways in which the question of unity has been addressed.

Consider first the problem of class alliances, an issue which has been at the centre of Marxist political debate in Europe. Here it is argued, especially by the European Communist Parties, that a necessary condition of effective socialist politics is the establishment of alliances between the working class and other popular classes and class fractions. Clearly, for any conception of class alliances to be proposed, one has to assume that the working class possesses minimal capacities as an agent; it must be organized, able to make calculations according to conditions and to recognize issues etc. This conception of 'working class agent' is, however, subject to serious problems.

Balibar, for example, discusses the question of alliances by directing critical attention to the PCF's notion of 'unity of the people' against monopoly capital. Contrary to PCF views, he argues that there is no evolutionary necessity leading to such unity. Rather, the outcome is dependent on 'practical struggle'. The way in which he conceives this struggle is significant, since he regards it as being between 'the revolutionary and counter-revolutionary forces in which the revolutionary forces — proletariat, peasantry and those manual or intellectual workers who are in the course of being absorbed into the proletariat — *must* exploit the contradictions of the class enemy' (Balibar, 1977, p. 116). Here, again, it is assumed that the working class has capacities of organization and leadership which rest upon its fundamental unity.

However, elsewhere Balibar presents a rather different argument, for he suggests that the strategy of the working class has to be the destruction of bourgeois class alliances which extend to within the proletariat itself. In this respect, the class unity of the proletariat is something which, contrary to the PCF, can never be spontaneously created (Balibar, 1977, p. 230).

What we are presented with here are two quite contradictory positions. On the one hand, the two major classes are regarded as unified entities with unambiguous class interests which constitute them as revolutionary and non-revolutionary forces. On the other hand, working class unity is recognized to be fundamentally problematic. In effect we are left with a strategy which is mere circularity; the condition of working class unity is the destruction by *it* of bourgeois class alliances. The working class is both unity (an 'it') and disunity. The resolution of proletarian *dis*unity is achieved by the co-ordinated actions of the proletariat—*as*—unity.

This theme of the working class as simultaneously unified and disunited recurs throughout Marxist political debate. Take, for example, the problem of the police. Reiner's consideration of this question is set by the general parameters of class analysis. In particular he is pre-occupied with the question of why the police consistently fail to adopt political positions sympathetic to the working class, given the working class background of many police officers. He begins by adopting the, by now familiar, pose of 'relative autonomy' as a solution to the gap between class determination and political practice. The place of the police in class relations does not determine their political position, but 'suggests the extent to which there is a basic identity of interests between the police and the working class. The question of identifying the class location of the police is not intended as a pigeon-holing exercise, but an exploration of political possibilities' (Reiner, 1978, p. 76). This passage reproduces the ambiguity already identified in Poulantzas, Wright and Balibar. On the one hand, it appears the class determination should define political practice. Hence, working class unity is assumed and the 'deviant' practice of the police is conceived as a problem with respect to such unity: 'if the police are essentially part of the working class it becomes hard to explain why they have been so much more consistently hostile to realizing their unity with it than almost any other section' (Reiner, 1978, p. 76). On the other hand, the recognition of such practice merely underlines that class location does not define it. Again we have the same contradiction that emerges in Balibar. The 'problem' can only be posed if the working class is regarded as a unity, but recognition of the problem simultaneously denies the fact of unity.

As in the case of Wright and Poulantzas, Reiner equips himself with a get-out clause. Class analysis, it seems, only indicates political possibility. Yet he, like these other authors, is entirely unconcerned with specifying concepts which would enable this seemingly crucial analysis of political possibility to be undertaken. In fact, his entire mode of approach denies this limited conception of class analysis. Like Poulantzas and Wright, Reiner, in the last resort, conceives all political ideologies and practices as manifestations of the dominant class relations under capitalism. In this, he almost directly echoes their view of politics: 'The position a group takes up in a concrete conjuncture must always be on one side or the other' (Reiner, 1978, p. 76).

A final example again illustrates the ambiguity surrounding the conception of 'working class as agent'. Allen has argued that the working class has to be treated as a unity or totality, though it is subject to internal variations in structure and practice. To the standard dichotomy of 'unity—disunity', Allen, however, adds a conceptual flourish. By recognizing the internal differentiation of the working class, he hopes to understand the 'contradictions' that exist within wage labour. For example, the consciousness and practice of dockers is a 'contradictory' phenomenon. They are solidaristic and militant yet, in their support for a movement like 'Powellism', display an attachment to racism. Other instances of 'contradiction' are, likewise, noted. For example, the Shotton steel managers supported workers in plants threatened with closure during the 1970s, despite a long identification with their employers. Allen concludes that such cases are evidence of the fact that 'all groups . . . adopt positions in the class struggle which are contradictory over time' (Allen, 1977, p. 77).

Allen's use of the term 'contradiction' is significant in this example, for it serves two purposes. First, it gives token recognition to 'deviant' forms of political practice, whilst avoiding the need to theorize the conditions of existence of such deviations, by labelling them (mere) 'contradictions'. Consequently, it enables the concept of 'working class as agent of politics' to be salvaged. Secondly, it enables specific forms of politics to be hived off to one or other side of the political division between capital and labour: why else should racism and industrial militancy be conceived as 'contradictory'?

It is apparent that the theme of 'unity—disunity' is merely another manifestation of Engels's dilemma of the 'more or less'. But these examples show more. *All* Marxists equate socialist politics with the attainment of genuine working class interest. The 'problem' of socialism is one of developing the conditions for such interests to be realized. Such a conception of politics, whatever its particular variation may be, therefore operates with the underlying assumption of a ready constituted working class interest to be achieved ('class unity').

But once the unity of classes in general, and of the working class in particular, is called into question, it follows that the concept of 'class interest' itself, rather than the problem of the means of its attainment, has to be called into doubt. The following chapter will consider this matter further by considering the Marxist treatment of political ideologies in the context of the problem of reductionism.

Class and political ideology: a non-reductionist solution?

Let us begin by considering how Marxism has perceived the relationship between two political ideologies, 'trades unionism' and 'socialism'. Unionism and socialism are placed together here for a particular reason. They are both regarded by Marxism as working class forms of politics. Because of this it is assumed that there is a necessary connection between them as types of political practice, the analysis of each being based upon the investigation of particular forms of working class interest and consciousness.

This much is made apparent in classical accounts of the two political forms. Lenin, for example, regards them as necessarily related by virtue of their common mediation by working class consciousness. In this respect, trades union 'spontaneism' represents nothing more than an 'embryonic form' of political consciousness proper — a recognition of immediate rather than fundamental interests (Lenin, 1902, p. 36). Each form of politics is equated with a variety of working class consciousness. The problem for Marxism is to translate one form into the other.

In view of this distinction between forms of class interest and corresponding forms of political practice, Marxist discussion of unionism tends to concentrate on its inherent limitations vis-à-vis socialism. Unionism has to be conceived in its necessary relationship to socialism because the fundamental agent of both is the working class. Unionism is, however, a lesser form of working class politics. It is 'an incomplete and deformed variant of class consciousness' (Anderson, 1967, p. 264). The world of unionist politics is 'an arena of limited class conflict' (Beynon, 1973, p. 105). What is being suggested in this sort of analysis, then, is that the effectiveness of each political form can be deduced from the quality of class interest which it is alleged to represent. 'Representation', in this case, is always mediated through the consciousness of the working class agent. (This is no less true of Lenin's analysis where consciousness, though dependent upon the intervention of an outside agent — the intelligentsia — is always mediated through the working class).

The conception of unionism and socialism as class-based political forms rests upon three propositions. First, that the working class is a political agent with class interests and a capacity for conscious realization of them. Secondly, that there is a form of practice called 'working class politics', unionism and socialism being variant forms of it. Thirdly, that such working class politics is ubiquitous because class conflict is itself ubiquitous. Here, Lenin argues that the unionist form of class conflict is inevitable (1902, p. 117), this being a corollary of the basic Marxist proposition that as long as there are classes there will be class conflict. In this view, then, the mere existence of the working class guarantees at least union struggle. At best, of course, it produces socialism.

All of these propositions are, however, called into doubt once the materialist conception of politics is questioned. For example, it is evident that that conception rests upon an ontology (the primacy of economic production) combined with a teleology (the tendential processes of economies, the concepts of historical transition etc.). Whereas ontology defines the agents of political practice as classes, teleology designates the parameters of the political activity; the problems which some classes pose, the solutions which others provide. In consequence, Marxism operates with a view of historically essential processes (such as socialism) being realized by essential agents (the working class). In the absence of those assumptions however, the concepts of 'class unity' and 'class interest' which are so basic to the materialist position have no justification.

This has serious repercussions for Marxist approaches to political calculation, for the reduction of politics to class conflict and the project of 'class analysis' which Marxists set themselves is only meaningful if these concepts can be sustained. Marxism's incarnation of socialism in the working class is *only* possible because the unity of that class is ultimately considered to have no determinate conditions of existence. For although Marxists may give practical recognition to the effectivity of political organization and ideology, materialist theory is constructed upon the assumption that class relations have priority over their political and ideological conditions of existence. In consequence, 'working class interest' or 'unity' can never be politically or ideologically called into existence. Instead, it has to be given as a (complex) necessary effect of capitalist relations.

One can find numerous examples from the 'classics' to support this view. It is not surprising, for example, that Marxists have never resolved the thorny problem of the relationship between class and party. Marx and Engels seem uncertain of how to tackle the question in the *Manifesto*. There, it is argued that the aim of the Communists is the 'formation of the proletariat into a class'. This would seem to be a clear indication of the effectivity of political theory and organization in the constitution of 'class interests' and 'class unity'. But then, it is immediately stated that Communist theory 'merely expresses . . . actual relations springing from an existing class struggle', a definite suggestion that working class action is subject to no such conditions of existence (Marx and Engels, 1848, p. 120).

Now, once it is granted that political and ideological forces (parties, pressure groups, institutions, etc.) are effective in the constitution of political interests, several consequences follow. For one thing, the prospects for socialism cannot be deduced from the structure of class relations. It is necessary to specify the conditions of existence of socialist politics, the issues around which it may be mobilized, the forms of organization it requires and so on. Furthermore, one question which has to be considered is the extent to which the concept of class is appropriate to a serious examination of these questions.

Our brief consideration of the Marxist analysis of trades unionism and socialism has suggested, however, a quite different mode of calculation. By assuming that there are two basic classes, Marxism has deduced that there are two basic forms of politics. Political ideologies can then be located with reference to one or other 'side' of the political arena. In the case of our example of 'working class politics', unionism may be regarded as a failure to realize socialism rather than as a specific form of politics which may — or may not according to circumstances — relate to socialism.

It is hardly surprising, then, that Marxist class analysis has remarkably little to say about socialism as a political ideology, or about the social and political conditions which might make for an effective socialist movement. More often than not socialism is theorized as a conjunction of structurally defined working class interest with working class political practice, through the mediation of class consciousness. Indeed, this theoretical assumption provides the rationale for class analysis itself. If the working class is the incarnation of socialism, then a correct definition of that class will itself constitute socialist political calculation.

In the case of 'working class politics', then, we seem to be confronted with the spectre of 'reductionism' again. Nevertheless, it might be maintained that the account of Marxist discourse presented here is a mere caricature. After all, is it not the case that, in the last decade, many Marxists have tried to move away from conceiving socialism as the inevitable product of an essential working class agent? Has there, moreover, not been a sustained attempt to resolve the problems of socialist political analysis by invoking a 'non-reductionist' solution?

The remainder of this chapter will consider three attempts to present a 'non-reductionist' solution to the problems of socialist politics in particular and ideology in general. Two of these examples (Przeworski, and Laclau and Mouffe) try to sustain a coherent materialist position. The third (Cutler *et al.*), though constituting a break with materialism, carries residues of the classical position, the effects of which require it to retain the problematic of 'reductionism/non-reductionism' within its conception of political calculation.

There are two justifications for considering these positions together. The first concerns the shared assumption that 'reductionism' is the fundamental obstacle which a theoretically adequate socialism has to resolve. It will be suggested here that that assumption is an inadequate one. The second concerns the fact that all of the authors are aware of the problematic nature of class formation and class agency. As a consequence of this they all see a resolution to the problems of reductionism beginning from an analysis of how the agents of socialist politics are constituted. Though this is a major theoretical advance, it is suggested here that none of these authors is able to resolve that question in a satisfactory manner.

The 'non-reductionist' solution to political ideology

Przeworski

One of the most interesting attempts to confront the problems of class analysis from within the materialist position is that of Przeworski. The significant advance which he makes on previous positions is to pose the question of the conditions of existence of class formation and to conceive such conditions of existence as forms of ideological and theoretical practice 'about' class.

In particular, it is argued that class formation cannot simply be regarded as given, but is always an 'effect of struggles'. In other words, economic, political and ideological conditions structure struggles, which have, as their effect, the 'organization', 'disorganization' and 'reorganization' of classes. This view rests upon four propositions. First, it is maintained that classes as actors are not objectively given, the relationship between class agents and relations of production being problematic. Secondly, classes are perceived as effects of struggles which are not uniquely determined by relations of production. Thirdly, class struggles are structured by the totality of economic, political and ideological relations and they have an autonomous effect on the process of class formation. Fourthly, given that struggles have an autonomous effect on formation, it follows that places in the relations of production can no longer define what classes will emerge in struggle.

What Przeworski is leading to in all of this is a quite specific and distinct conception of class analysis, one which no longer derives political and ideological practices from 'objective' class locations, but instead regards the classification of these positions as 'imminent to the practices that (may) result in class formation'. In other words, 'the very theory of classes must be viewed as internal to particular political projects' (Przeworski, 1977, p. 367). What this indicates is that positions in the relations of production are not to be considered as 'objective' and 'prior' to class struggle. Instead, they are 'objective only to the extent to which they make the particular projects historically realizable or not' (Przeworski, 1977, p. 367).

Przeworski's advantages over others should be obvious. For one thing he explodes the myth that class interests are an unproblematic and objective basis for collective action. Rightly, he points to the fact that capitalist relations of production provide a number of *alternative* bases for political action. There is, in other words, just as much an 'objective' basis for proletarian hostility to the 'welfare' or 'lumpen' class, as there is for hostility towards capital — and indeed there may be more. At best, he suggests that the fact that wage labourers share the common experience of separation from the means of production provides them with some communality of interests. But this is by no means sufficient to constitute class interest pure and simple, for within such communality, the basis of such political interests can be broadened or narrowed by a variety of 'strategies of class formation' (Przeworski, 1977, p. 401), the important point being that such strategies will be effective in the constitution of class interests and formation. For this reason Przeworski is adamant that class is not a datum prior to struggle. Rather, ideological and political struggles are struggles *about* class before they are struggles *among* classes. More to the point, he seeks to establish class analysis firmly within political and ideological problems and practices to which its pertinence has to be established by theoretical endeavour rather than derived from ontological primacy. Any suggestion of a simple link between class analysis and political calculation is totally rejected.

But we have also indicated that Przeworski remains faithful to the materialist conception of politics and it is necessary now to consider what form this adherence takes and what effect it has on his attempt to reformulate the relationship between classes and politics.

Broadly speaking, Przeworski's materialism is expressed in two related aspects. First, he says that, given his stated position on the fundamentally problematic status of the class concept, an obvious question arises: why should questions about the membership of classes in struggle, the consequences of particular struggles and the interests of those participating, be posed with respect to a 'broadly defined system of *production*'? Why not race, religion, nationality or any other potential strategic sphere? That is to say, if ideological and political relations are effective and no less 'objective' than relations of production, why not define 'classes' in these terms?

His response to this question is, by his own admission, 'rudimentary' and 'incomplete'. What it amounts to is a simple claim that such an emphasis may be justified by the priority which the author affords to historical development as lawfully directed by the development of the productive forces and capital accumulation. The justification therefore rests upon an adoption of the materialist ontology and teleology. The theoretical effects of this type of assumption are prominent in a second aspect of the analysis, the adoption of the conception of the social formation as 'totality'.

The consequences of that adoption are by no means as obvious as in some of the authors discussed previously. The clear merit of Przeworski's argument lies in his recognition of the problematic nature of the Marxist conception of class agency. Instead of proposing the existence of classes as unconditional forces, it is argued that the problem has to be re-thought in a number of specific respects. First, class formation has to be posed as a strategy internal to particular political projects. Such formation is not merely 'given' by the presence of any 'objective' social relations. Secondly, given that such formation is dependent on specific forms of political theory and practice, its existence is clearly subject to the effects of antagonism within these spheres. Class formation is, therefore, a political practice involving the possible 'organization', 'disorganization' and 'reorganization' of classes. Thirdly and in accordance with this, class formation is subject to the effects of specific economic, political and ideological conditions, such conditions having effectivity in that same 'organization', 'disorganization' and 'reorganization' of classes.

Now these three propositions appear to be a far cry from the conventional Marxist approach to political class analysis discussed in Chapter 6. Contrary to such conventions, Przeworski is seeking to designate class formation as subject to the effects of definite theoretical and social conditions — conditions which are genuinely effective, rather than merely 'overdetermined'. But the promise contained within this project remains sadly unrealized.

The reason for this failure can be traced to the author's adoption of the ontology ('priority' of production) and teleology ('lawfulness' of development) of classical materialism and his utilization of these in conceptualizing theoretical and social conditions. Such conditions are, in fact, conceived as instances of the capitalist 'totality of economic, political and ideological relations' (see Przeworski, 1977, pp. 368, 373, 377). This has clear effects at the level of substantive analysis. Take, for example, the attempt to specify the forms of organization of social relations in capitalist democracies which constitute the 'objective conditions' under which social movements 'develop their practices of class formation' (Przeworski, 1977, pp. 373—7). What is claimed here is that the totality of economic, political and ideological relations under capitalism structures socialist politics in particular directions. For example, the bourgeoisie has the capacity to reproduce social relations in their 'phenomenal' forms so that individuals are reproduced as students, Roman Catholics ... anything other than as occupants of class positions.

But this hardly fits in with the view that class formation is subject to social conditions, for here we have a class agent or force (the bourgeoisie) that derives its capacities, not from determinate social conditions, but from the structure of social relations in the capitalist totality. In fact, Przeworski looks, not at the effects of determinate social conditions, but at the allegedly necessary consequences of an unconditional unity of capitalist relations. This has to lead to the peculiar implication that class formation is *only* a problem for the proletariat. The bourgeoisie, on the contrary, is already and always constituted as an effective political force because of its derivation from the structure of social relations within the capitalist totality. This, in turn, undermines the proposition that the politics of class formation is dependent on definite *theoretical* strategies. Theoretical calculation appears only to be necessary to socialist politics. Capitalist politics is without theoretical or social conditions of existence.

It should be clear that Przeworski's attempt to remedy the problems of Marxist class analysis is unsuccessful. Despite his genuine recognition of the inadequacies of the classical position, such recognition is rendered ineffectual by the retention of the materialist conception of politics. All that he achieves is the partial transference of the 'objective' political destiny of classes to the level of the instances of the social formation/ totality. But this merely reproduces the same 'reductionism' he had set out to avoid.

Laclau and Mouffe

Laclau and Mouffe's solution to the problem of reductionism begins from an attempt to refine the work of Gramsci. Towards this end, the concept of hegemony is regarded as crucial, since it points us towards a new theory of the unity of the social formation. Rather than conceiving unity as the result of a processual teleology, we are told that it depends upon 'political articulations' resulting from 'the relation between antagonistic social forces' (Laclau and Mouffe, 1981, p. 20). Hegemony, it is said, enables us to analyse social relations and address the problem of the constitution of social agents involved in them.

Much of the intention behind this project is laudable. For example, the authors rightly point to the failure of 'the traditional discourse of Marxism, centred on the class struggle and the analysis of economic contradictions' to deal with new political subjects such as 'women, national, racial and sexual minorities, anti-nuclear and anti-institutional movements'. Moreover, both are fully aware of the contradictions within Marxist discourse. For example, Marx himself sees class struggle as both an active process and as a structural corollary of the development of the forces of production. Indeed, the history of Marxism has been 'marked by the presence of these two contradictory discourses' (Laclau and Mouffe, 1981, p. 17).

For Laclau and Mouffe twentieth-century Marxism involves a series of complex and partial breaks with the economistic tradition. Leninism is characterized both as a break with the economism of the Second International and an affirmation of its theoretical dominance. In effect, it is suggested that Lenin resolves the problem of Marxism's incapacity to deal with the increasing importance of the 'superstructure' by invoking the 'primacy of the political'. That solution is, however, a practical rather than a theoretical one, Lenin resolving a theoretical problem at the level of political practice (Mouffe, 1979, p. 176). In this respect, Mouffe sees Gramsci's work as as attempt to extract the theoretical consequences of Leninist political practice. According to this view, Gramsci may be seen as the instigator of an embryonic non-reductionist theory, though the theoretical status of his work remains rudimentary: 'a radically anti-economistic problematic of ideology is *operating in the practical state* in Gramsci's conception of hegemony' (Mouffe, 1979, p. 178, emphasis added).

Although Gramsci makes major advances, then, for political and intellectual reasons (imprisonment, the limitations of Croce's historicism) he ·fails to provide theoretically adequate solutions. For example, he makes an important advance in recognizing the material nature of ideology, but is unable to formulate a theory of the mechanisms by which ideological practice 'consists in the production of subjects' (Mouffe, 1979, p. 188).

What is required, then, according to Laclau and Mouffe, is a refinement of Gramscian Marxism through a further development of the concept of hegemony. This will inevitably lead to a 'Copernican revolution' in Marxist theory (Laclau and Mouffe, 1981, p. 17). It is towards such a theoretical revolution that their own work is directed and one of the most significant points of departure of that work is the attempt to address the question of the constitution of subjects of social relations in a non-reductionist manner.

There appear to be two types of solution to the problems of reductionism and social agency in Laclau and Mouffe, though how far they can be called distinct positions, given their overlap, is open to question. The first of these positions can be traced to Mouffe's analysis of Gramsci's concept of hegemony. Here, she outlines the dimensions of Gramsci's embryonic non-reductionism and sets out to impose a 'symptomatic reading' on it (Mouffe, 1979, p. 170). This produces a dualistic emphasis. Hegemony is seen as a sphere of political struggle involving forces which are irreducible to classes. Yet this recognition is combined with the view that only a 'fundamental class' can be hegemonic. Thus, Mouffe insists that hegemony involves more than mere 'class alliances', but is equally adamant that the plurality of ideologies that comprise the hegemonic terrain are gathered into discernible 'ensembles'.

In view of what has been said in previous chapters, the effect of this combination should be obvious. On the one hand, we have an affirmation of the irreducibility of politics and ideology to class relations; ideologies are not coherent class packages; decisive elements in ideological struggle are of a non-class nature (e.g. national and popular elements). On the other hand, Mouffe has to elucidate a theory of 'ensemblement', given her insistence that irreducible ideological elements do take on a class belonging: 'these elements do not in themselves express class interests, but . . . their class character is conferred upon them by the discourse to which they are articulated and by the type of subject thus created' (Mouffe, 1979, p. 195).

At this stage Mouffe's analysis simply has recourse to an elaborate version of 'economic determination in the last instance', whereby the class belonging of ideologies is a product of the dominance of discourses which are themselves class-based. This position allows Mouffe to avoid the attribution of a necessary class belonging to all ideological elements, but only by virtue of a reaffirmation of complex economism. Hence, the ideological 'ensembles' which contain autonomous elements are located in the 'fundamental classes' (Mouffe, 1979, p. 200).

A second version of Laclau and Mouffe's position seems potentially more fruitful. For one thing, the constitution of social agents is recognized to be a problem for consideration. Indeed, the concept of hegemony is regarded as 'a process of production of subjects' (Laclau and Mouffe, 1981, p. 20). According to this view, hegemony is said to be discursively constituted, the 'discursive' in this case comprising the 'social' *per se*, rather than a mere level or superstructure within a totality dominated by the primacy of economic class relations (Laclau, 1980a, p. 87).

The claim that social agents and relations are constituted in and through discourse is combined with two other emphases. First, there is a refusal to endow class agency with any form of primacy. Thus, in the case of socialist politics, the working class has no necessary hegemonic function. Indeed, class conflict is discursively constituted rather than derived from extra-discursive relations or ontological principles. Secondly, Laclau and Mouffe move from an adoption of economic determination in the last instance to an affirmation of the 'primacy of politics', even in the sphere of the economy itself (Laclau and Mouffe, 1981, p. 22). The economy, like all other spheres of society, is, then, to be conceived as an arena of struggle for hegemony. Such hegemonic/political or discursive primacy rests, however, upon no ontological assumptions about the structure of the social formation:

> To affirm the priority of the discursive implies proposing a theoretical perspective in the analysis of society as a whole; it does not involve an *a priori* commitment to any theoretical position on the articulation of levels within that society. (Laclau, 1980a, p. 87)

How successful, then, is this attempt to invoke discursive priority as a means of theorizing social agents/relations in a non-reductionist form?

Laclau and Mouffe's work gives rise to three categories of problem. The first is similar to that arising in Przeworski's analysis. Despite their denial of the primacy of class relations and their insistence on the discursive constitution of social agents, they perceive socialist politics as a struggle for the attainment of unity amongst diverse social groups whose common interest resides in their 'anti-capitalist' character. What is at issue here is not the desirability of uniting women, blacks, anti-nuclear campaigners and the like, but the 'capitalism' which confronts them. To perceive such movements as merely 'new contradictions' (Laclau and Mouffe, 1981, p. 17) facing an enduring capitalism is to refuse to pose the problem of the discursive constitution of *capitalist* social relations. Despite the authors' insistence on the centrality of hegemonic struggle, there is an uncomfortable sense in which capitalism is perceived as a totality facing a disparate socialist and popular movement. And even where attempts are made to specify means where ideological 'ensembles' emerge that underpin bourgeois hegemony, the result is unconvincing. (Witness Laclau's remarkably complicated attempt to theorize modes of hegemonic discourse in 1980a, p. 90ff. Here, complexity cannot obscure the fact that such modes are, in Jessop's phrase, 'inter-discursive', in so far as they are polarized around *pre*-discursive ideological ensembles located in fundamental classes.)

A second set of problems arise at the strategic level. It is significant that much neo-Gramscian debate has concerned itself with the problems of democracy, equality and participation vis-à-vis the complex of political interest groups which are incorporated under the umbrella of 'the left'. Now there is nothing wrong with socialists 'taking democracy seriously', but the manner in which the problem is posed sometimes creates difficulties of its own. Mouffe's 'defence of democracy' (1981, pp. 231–3) is concerned not with democracy as such, but with its potential for uniting the 'fragments' of the left.

> It is sometimes said that there is no basis for a unity between the different parts of the democratic movement. Indeed at first sight their demands seem so different . . . that without postulating a pre-given unity . . . it might appear very difficult to justify the assertion that unity can and should be built. Nevertheless one can recognize the presence of a common element

because all those demands are in some way or other the expression of a struggle for equality and participation and against oppression and exclusion. (Mouffe, 1981, pp. 232–3)

What is significant here is the verbal slippage which occurs in the course of the argument. Pre-given unity is denied at one level (class) only to be resurrected at another; it is assumed that the 'fragments' are parts of a democratic movement, the source of whose potential unity derives from their confrontation with 'non-democratic' forces of 'oppression and exclusion'. The terms have changed but the assumptions remain the same. And what is even more striking is the strategic emptiness of all this. 'Democratic unity', though sounding more 'concrete' and less problematic than 'class unity', obscures the need to discuss actual political issues and programmes around which unity may or may not be constructed.

A third problem arises as a consequence of the attempt to give primacy to the discursive and thereby reject the privileging of classes. Initially, it seems that Laclau regards the question of *which* social agents contest the terrain of hegemony as a problem for consideration, for hegemony, he insists, is much more than 'a political confluence between pre-constituted social agencies' (1980b, p. 254).

However, the denial of any privileging of class does not extend to the question of class agency itself. Laclau's denial of 'pre-constitution' is combined with the assumption that at least some of the agents of hegemonic struggle are classes. The problem which Laclau and Mouffe pose for themselves concerns the capacities of classes and non-class agents to contest effectively for hegemony. In one sense, this amounts to a denial of the privileging of classes; hegemony is more than a contest between the fundamental classes since it is also a location for intervention by non-class forces. But in another sense class remains privileged, since no attempt is made to question the assumption that classes *are* constituted as agents of hegemonic conflict. The debate about 'primacy' and 'privileging' is a debate directed towards the problem of how classes relate to non-class forces, not a debate about classes *qua* agents.

Despite their insistence on discursive primacy, Laclau and Mouffe fail to accept the logical force of their own theoretical protocols. By virtue of this failure, they choose not to address an obvious question. Are classes social and political agents? If so, in what sense are they agents? If not, why not?

Despite their promise to address the question of the constitution of social agents Laclau and Mouffe fail to pay any critical attention to the concept of class itself. Indeed, some of their comments show a remarkable lack of understanding of the implications of their own arguments and objectives. For example, Laclau tells us that 'the working class constitutes itself as a hegemonic force to the extent that it ceases to be a mere economic agent with specific interests and becomes a complex popular subject' (1980b, p. 256). The shortcomings of this comment are obvious. For one thing it reproduces, yet again, the theoretical sterility of the classical dualisms (class in itself/class for itself; trades union consciousness/political consciousness; immediate interests/fundamental interests). For another, it rests upon the unfounded assumption that classes comprise (even) economic agents, let alone political ones.

Ultimately, then, Laclau and Mouffe are unwilling to apply the criterion of discursive primacy to the object of class itself. Far from being the radical departure which it seems, their work remains within the confines of debates about the relative autonomy of class and non-class forces in hegemonic struggle. Let us now consider a third attempt to pose the problem of class agency.

Cutler, Hindess, Hirst and Hussain

Cutler *et al.* present a rigorous and detailed critique of the theoretical structure of classical Marxism. Two elements of that critique are particularly important. The first is their rejection of the concept of 'mode of production' and certain of the propositions associated with it — notably the teleological principal of causality that goes with the concept of 'total social capital' and its 'laws of motion'. The second is their rejection of the Marxist ontology and its associated concept of 'determination in the last instance' by the economy.

These views enable the authors to cast doubt upon the classical Marxist conception of the social totality. Given their rejection of the rationalistic epistemology upon which such a conception is based (Cutler *et al.*, 1977, pp. 211–12, 313), they propose to define a social formation, not as a social totality, but as a 'set of relations of production together with the economic, political and cultural forms in which their conditions of existence are secured'. They insist, however, that there is no necessity for such conditions of existence to be secured and no necessary structure of the social formation in which relations and forms must be combined (Cutler *et al.*, 1977, p. 224).

The claim that connections between economic and political or cultural relations should be conceived in terms of 'conditions of existence' rather than 'determination' and 'causality' — indeed the authors reject all general theories of causality — rests upon the rejection of the 'rationalist conception of discourse' and the strategies of 'privileging' associated with it (Cutler *et al.*, 1977, pp. 5, 124ff; see also Hindess and Hirst, 1977). Instead, the authors adopt the principle of 'discursive primacy', refusing to analyse the social formation in terms of some allegedly essential structure of social relations and arguing merely for the 'posing of problems' for analysis. The problems of socialist politics are, then, considered to be constructed rather than deduced from some essential structure of reality. For example, all attempts to see political and ideological relations as 'personifications' of class relations are rejected. Instead, it is emphasized that there are no 'socialist' issues *per se*, assigned as 'socialist' by class interests, for socialism is always and only a political ideology (Cutler *et al.*, 1978, p. 258).

Now it is obvious that the present text owes a considerable debt to the work of Cutler *et al.* and the force of their general argument is, in our view, entirely correct. There are, however, two specific areas of their argument which require more detailed consideration and criticism. The first of these concerns their analysis and critique of class agency and the second, their resolution to the problem of reductionism.

With regard to the question of classes, the authors adopt two critical propositions. First, class relations are granted discursive priority in socialist politics: 'The analysis of economic class relations provides the starting point of socialist political calculation' (Cutler *et al.*, 1977, p. 318). Secondly, it is emphasized that such priority is only discursive. Politics and ideology are not to be regarded as processes contained within an essential class conflict. Indeed, it is suggested that 'when we examine political and ideological struggles we find state apparatuses, political parties and organizations, demonstrations and riotous mobs, bodies of armed men, newspapers and magazines etc., but we do not find *classes* lined up against each other' (Cutler *et al.*, 1977, p. 232).

What is, in fact, indicated here is the need for a new approach to the analysis of social agency, an approach where agents and relations are conceived in terms of their determinate conditions of existence (see especially Cutler *et al.*, 1977, ch. 11). Since it is denied that there are any universal or essential agents/relations it has to be maintained that all are specific and irreducible. For this reason, those positions which regard classes as socio-political agents are unacceptable. Likewise, the classical view that economic and social agents personify or represent class relations is deemed untenable. Indeed, it is continually emphasized that it is *specific* economic agents of possession or separation which take decisions and act. Such action has its own effectivity and cannot be considered a product of outside 'structural' determinants imposed on the calculating agent: 'If calculation by capitalists does have an effectivity then the capitalist cannot be reduced to the personification of capital' (Cutler *et al.*, 1977, p. 265). According to this view, economic calculation will have determinate conditions of existence in law, politics, culture and the like, but such conditions do not constitute the totality ('structured in dominance') whereby Marxists conceive action as a personification of the agent's class location.

In consequence of this denial of class essentialism, the authors use a particular formula to define classes, for we are told that 'classes are categories of economic agents' (Cutler *et al.*, 1977, p. 169 *passim*). Now despite the fact that a coherent and consistent definition of class is obviously crucial for a text which gives priority to the 'problem of class relations', this formula turns out to be something of an enigma. Initially, we are told that classical Marxism itself conceives classes in this way (Cutler *et al.*, 1977, p. 169), but this is clearly impossible to sustain. Marx uses the term 'category' to convey precisely the opposite meaning from that put forward here. For Marx, individuals 'are the personifications of economic categories, embodiments of particular class relations and class interests' (Marx, 1867, p. xix). In this case, class does constitute a 'category', but that category comprises a 'structure' which determines the nature of all social relations (economic determination in the last instance) and accounts for all of the specific actions of particular agents. Thus, capitalists are personifications of that 'category' called the capitalist class.

The utilization of the 'category formula' by Cutler *et al.* turns out to involve a direct rebuttal of such a conception of social agency. Where Marx regards categories of classes as fundamental socio-political agents, they use the term in a quite different sense. Far from implying class agency, the term 'category' serves as a direct denial of it. It is because classes comprise specific categories of agents that the very specificity and irreducibility of their action can be guaranteed. For Cutler *et al.* it is specific economic agents of possession and separation which act and take decisions. The classes into which such agents are 'categorized' are mere repositories. It is not the class which has effectivity in formulating action and decision but the specific agent and its social conditions of existence.

But once this is admitted the pertinence of the concept of 'class relations' as a basic 'problem' for analysis and 'starting point for socialist political calculation' becomes open to question. Classes, we are told, are categories of agents, but in a very real sense the term 'category' is intended to convey nothing at all. The category formula serves to *deny* the effectivity of class at the level of social action whilst *reaffirming* it as the central problem of socialist politics. The impossibility of this combination of views leads Cutler *et al.* to be continually ambiguous in their theorization of the object 'class relations'. For example, despite their strictures about Marxism's denial of the specificity of agents in its conceptualization of classes, they still insist on making repeated reference to the 'structure of economic class relations'. Precisely what this means in the context of an argument which entirely rejects 'structural determination' is unclear. A further example indicates the problem even more clearly. It is said that economic class relations 'presuppose the existence of political struggles whose outcome has differential effects *on the precise relations of the classes or particular categories of agents within them*' (Cutler *et al.*, 1977, p. 241, emphasis added). This comment signifies the ambivalence of the category formula.

Are class relations to be conceived as relations between 'classes' or are they simply relations between determinate economic agents? If the former, then the category formula is redundant. If the latter and if no effectivity is to be attached to the term 'class' in the determination of action, then that term is redundant.

The employment of the category formula is therefore intended to deny class agency but the very retention of the problem of class relations has to imply some sort of effectivity to the class concept vis-à-vis the agents that occupy places in the class structure, or be meaningless. One cannot simultaneously give class relations discursive priority in socialist political calculation and deny these relations effectivity in economic, political and ideological practice. 'Class relations' as a concept is meaningless unless it is able to designate classes as agents. Indeed, this conclusion has to follow from the way that Cutler *et al.* (rightly) theorize the concept of *agent* as a locus of social action in a social *relation*, emphasizing the interdependence of the two: 'The interdependence of the concepts of agent and social relation ensures that no conceptualization of one is possible without at least some implicit conceptualization of the other' (1977, p. 267).

The discursive prioritizing of class relations in socialist politics reaffirms the interdependence of this concept with that of class agency despite the authors' attempts to deny that interdependence in the category formula. The fact is that if one wants to replace structural determination and class essentialism by an analysis of social agency in terms of conditions of existence, one cannot retain the concept of class relations *in any theoretically rigorous sense*. If the specificity of social relations, forms of calculation and practices is to be proposed, the concept of class relations is inadequate as a 'starting point' for socialist politics. Despite the provision of a rigorous set of concepts for the denial of class agency and the reconceptualizing of social agents/relations, Cutler *et al.*, in retaining the concept of class relations, are forced to make 'at least some implicit conceptualization of the other'.

The theoretical consequences of this retention of a conception of class agency are seen most clearly in the authors' attempt to address the problem of reductionism. They consider this to be one of the central problems of Marxism and, in some respects, the dominant problem of their text concerns the question of how to produce a correct theory of the 'class/politics relation'.

In the authors' view the problem of reductionism in classical Marxism involves 'reconciling a conception of classes as categories of economic agents, and as political forces with a non-reductionist conception of politics' (Cutler *et al.*, 1977, p. 183). Two points need to be made here. In the first place, let us merely observe that since Marxism does not conceive classes as 'categories' in the sense intended here, such a view of reductionism cannot strictly be attributed to Marxism. The second point is, however, more important. What needs to be considered here is the consequence of the adoption of the category formula of class for the question of reductionism. Let us begin by assuming, for argument's sake, that classes *are* 'categories of economic agent' (i.e., that the formula actually has a coherent meaning). For that matter, let us even suppose that Marxism conceives classes in this sense. What, then, are the effects of these assumptions for posing and resolving the problem of reductionism?

With regard to this issue, the authors suggest a general proposition is basic to the understanding of the problem: 'If classes are conceived as categories of economic agent then they cannot also be conceived as political or cultural agents' (Cutler *et al.*, 1977, p. 231).

But in the light of what has been said already this proposition is decidedly peculiar, for what the category formula has sought to establish is that classes are not agents at all. To paraphrase the above proposition: 'If classes are conceived as categories of economic agent, then they cannot be conceived as agents and, in consequence, the "problem of reductionism" *cannot arise*'. The posing of the problem of reductionism in the context of the category formula is, therefore, a non sequitur. If classes are categories of agents there is no problem of reductionism.

In fact, this continued involvement with the question of reductionism arises because of their retention of the problem of class relations. The decision to attach discursive priority to that problem has the effect of conjuring up a necessary conception of class agency. The problem of reductionism can then be resolved by distancing political and economic agents from class agents.

Indeed, there is more to it than this, for it is evident that the adoption of an implicit conception of class agency signals a partial recall of the problematic of society as 'totality'. That this is the case can be shown by indicating the proposed solution to the problem of reductionism. This solution amounts to the attempt to establish 'the field of politics itself' (Cutler *et al.*, 1977, p. 312), by rigorously demarcating politics from class relations. In effect, the specificity of political and ideological agents/relations is achieved by an insistence upon their demarcation as phenomena. Anything less than such a demarcation leads, in the authors' view, to reductionism. The solution is, then, a predictable one. One has to turn the classical Marxist position on its head. Instead of a correspondence or relative correspondence between the economic and the political spheres, they invoke a 'non correspondence'. Or, to put it another way, 'relative autonomy' gives way to 'autonomy':

> There is no necessary general correspondence between economic classes and the forces articulated in political struggle. This general non correspondence does not exclude the possibility of specific relations. (Cutler *et al.*, 1978, p. 257)

Apart from the semantic confusion presented here — the equation of 'no necessary correspondence' with 'necessary non correspondence' — which may be ignored for present purposes, the solution amounts to a simple reversal of the Marxist position. Politics is not determined, it is autonomous. But to pose the problem of politics in this manner is simply to re-enter the domain of circularity and speculation which Cutler *et al.* did so much to break down. For the solution readopts problems and propositions which have *already* been superseded elsewhere in the text. In particular, claims concerning the autonomy of the 'field of politics' have no place in a discourse which proposes to argue 'that the connections between economic, political and cultural relations and practices must be conceptualized not in terms of determination and causality but rather in terms of conditions of existence and the forms in which they may be realized' (Cutler *et al.*, 1977, p. 131). Yet what we are confronted with is a false dichotomy: 'Either economism or the non-correspondence of political forces and economic classes' (Hirst, 1977, p. 131).

Such a conception of the problems of political calculation is, however, only feasible in a discourse which continues to pursue at one level the objective of correctly identifying 'general–causal' mechanisms ('no necessary general correspondence'). That ambiguous objective is itself contingent upon a theory which continues to flirt with the framework of society as totality, despite providing some of the means for rejecting that framework. Yet it is only because of its residual adoption of that assumption that the 'class/politics relation' (the relationship between two fields or levels of the totality) can be posed as a problem and 'anti-reductionism' be presented as a general solution to it.

In the last resort, Cutler *et al.* are forced back into a position which merely turns classical Marxism on its head. Whatever the novelty of this new 'general' solution however, it cannot resolve the problems of speculativeness and incoherence which their own analysis has shown all such general theories to exhibit. Despite the real value of their work this particular part of their analysis produces an incoherent solution (the establishment of the 'field' of politics) to a false problem (how to arrive at a non-reductionist analysis of the 'class/politics relation'). Let us now consider both the status of the 'problem of reductionism' and the utility of the class concept itself.

Theoretical and Political Conclusions

8

Socialist theory and socialist pluralism

In this final chapter summary comments will be made on the four main areas which the analysis has addressed; reductionism; class analysis; economic and social agency; the state. The last of these areas provides the basis for a short discussion of socialist political intervention and what is termed 'socialist pluralism'.

The 'problem of reductionism'

Chapter 7 examined a number of attempts to pose the problem of socialist politics through a problematic of 'reductionism v. non-reductionism'. What we need to do at this stage is to identify the phenomenon reductionism, for there is invariably an assumption in Marxism that its meaning is both precise and precisely understood.

One thing which is striking is that the variety of complex 'solutions' to the problem of reductionism stand in stark contrast to the simplistic manner in which the problem is perceived. The general assumption is that the problem is obvious. Reductionist Marxisms generate theoretically inadequate analyses and inappropriate or erroneous strategic directives. On that much, everybody appears to agree.

That conception of reductionism is, however, difficult to square with the evidence of previous chapters. If anything has been revealed in these chapters it is that reductionism, as a problem, is somewhat enigmatic. To begin with, the materialist conception of politics itself consists of a combination of reductionist and non-reductionist elements — the 'more or less' of Engels's concept of representation. The effects of this are illustrated in the various instances discussed; Marx's attempt to regard communist theory as both a condition of class formation and an effect of class struggle; the various attempts to deduce political lessons from class analysis, coupled with the inability to fix any cohesive political attachments to the classes analysed, and so on.

That this should be so is hardly surprising. We have seen that the materialist conception of politics, by combining incompatible forms of determination is able to produce a conceptual and strategic space. This space allows for the emergence of a 'non-reductionist theory' ('relative autonomy', 'dialectics', 'economic determination in the last instance', 'form-determined mediation', call it what you will) and, indeed, may sanction 'non-reductionist' forms of intervention at the level of political practice. We have seen, however, that 'non-reductionism' is merely the sign of an absence. It cannot provide a theoretical solution to the irreconcilable determinations which underpin it. Indeed, such strategic interventions which are proposed are invariably arbitrary vis-à-vis the 'materialism' which they are alleged to represent. The irony is that in a discourse which is dubbed 'deterministic' by its critics, there should so often be an *indeterminate* relationship between the theoretical structure it advances and the political interventions it makes.

The problem is not, then, reductionist practice, so much as the effects of the problematic of reductionism *v.* non-reductionism. To be specific, the problem is the limitation which that problematic has placed on the parameters of socialist thinking. In particular, an effective socialist politics has, mistakenly, been seen to depend upon a general, non-reductionist solution to the problem of the 'class-politics' relation.

The suggestion that the problematic of reductionism *v.* non-reductionism has to be dispensed with, rather than 'resolved', conflicts with most current versions of socialist theory. In order to support this suggestion further, let us reconsider that problematic.

The non-reductionist solution to economistic Marxism aims to establish a mode of analysis which can recognize the 'specificity' of political, cultural and ideological relations vis-à-vis economic classes. However, the problem of specificity can only be posed and non-reductionism invoked as a solution to it, if certain assumptions are adopted. In all of the positions so far discussed, two broad, though by no means mutually exclusive, sets of assumptions have been distinguishable, each providing a basis for establishing the specificity of politics.

The first of these is a broadly structural emphasis where society is conceived as a totality or unity of 'levels', 'forms' or 'instances', each constituent element being a 'relatively autonomous' component of the whole. Here, the specificity of each element both underlies and emphasizes the ultimate unity of the totality. According to this view, the structure of any society-totality is governed by general ontological and teleological principles of organization so that each element has a place given specifically to it. In consequence, a general account of the relationship between any two or more elements (say class and politics) is possible, the specificity of any single element being explained by virtue of general principles of organization (e.g. determination in the last instance by the economy; for a discussion of some of the similarities between this view and that of the classical structural sociologies, see Johnston, 1981).

If the isolation of elements within 'society as totality' represents one mode of theorizing the specificity of politics, a second method concentrates on the attempt to define it as a specific form of action. According to this view politics may be regarded as a form of human activity which is either (more or less) unconditional or (more or less) conditional. In so far as the latter is proposed and such action is deemed to have 'conditions of existence', these are to be conceived in terms of a polarization of 'objective' structure with 'subjective' human action.

The classical expression of this theory of politics is found in Weberian sociology which assumes a definite ontology (the primacy of subjective action) and teleology (the derivation of social relations from subjective orientations to action). But it should be apparent that the polarization of structure and action is by no means peculiar to sociological discourses. Marxism's attempt to analyse the relationship of economic classes and politics is one which operates simultaneously at two levels. On the one hand, an attempt is made to theorize the relationship between two unitary elements of the social totality (class and politics). On the other hand, that analysis is mediated by the concept of class consciousness, whereby the ontologically defined 'objective' interests that comprise class unity are set against the teleological means of their ever-potential realization in subjectively conscious political action.

It should be apparent from what has been said here that these two sets of assumptions, far from being incompatible, are mutually supportive. For instance, Chapter 3 has shown, through the example of the corporation, that 'structuralist' assumptions depend upon a conception of action which invokes subjective essentialism, since categories of subjects ('persons') are essential to the process of 'personification'. (This example also shows, incidentally, that subjectivism is not peculiar to those Marxisms which invoke class consciousness).

The Marxist analysis of politics, therefore, inevitably centres upon the question of how far 'structure' determines 'action' or vice versa. But there are serious grounds for asking whether this polarization is inevitable or necessary. The suggestion made in Chapter 3 – and reconsidered below – that social agency is not reducible to subjective action provides a potential means of avoiding the traditional dichotomy of structure *v.* action and determination *v.* (relative) autonomy.

Moreover, in the absence of ontology and teleology, the problem of the relative determination of action – to which non-reductionism may be proposed as a solution – cannot be sustained. For if it is denied that society is a totality, there can be no general theory of the social ensemblement, nor of the specificity of any single element within it (e.g., the British state). Indeed, what previous chapters have shown is that there can be no general (non-reductionist) solution to the problems of socialist politics. The theoretical objectives which Marxists have set themselves are impossible ones.

The problematic of reductionism *v.* non-reductionism is rejected, then, not for any reductive analysis it 'produces', but for the same reasons that the ontology and teleology which underlie it are rejected. No single set of social relations can be regarded as having necessary primacy in political analysis. It cannot be argued that there are any essential or fundamental political problems deriving unconditionally from some ontologically defined source. Nor can it be maintained that there are any essential agents, whether individuals or classes, through which necessary processes or forms of action are teleologically realized or realizeable.

It is suggested here that the denial of the classical problematic enables certain issues to be addressed which have hitherto been foreclosed (the non-unitary state, the non-human agent, corporate possession and so on). But, in claiming this, it is apparent that socialist discourse may, in consequence, have to be radically transformed. We will consider some of these questions and their possible implications below, but first, let us return to another central issue of our discussion, the question of class.

Socialism and 'class politics'

In Chapter 6 it was shown that the concept of class interest is problematic. Though recognizing working class disunity at the level of practical politics, Marxism continues to regard socialism as the realization of an essence (working class interest) beyond the practical. In effect, this amounts to a failure to theorize socialist politics and ideology. Though, as we suggested in Chapter 7, some writers are aware of the problematic nature of class agency, there remains considerable equivocation over the status of classes in socialist politics. Perhaps the clearest example of this occurs in Cutler *et al.* where class agency is denied at the level of action and decision-making only to be re-inserted via 'discursive priority' as the central problem for socialist politics.

It is by no means clear, then, what place class has in socialist politics, nor indeed, whether it has a serious place at all. What has been indicated in previous chapters, however, is that the content of socialist politics, the issues around which it may be mobilized and the character of the agents which participate in it, are problems which require serious consideration. So far, neither Marxist nor non-Marxist socialists have given these questions much thought.

That is not to say that they have not been considered at all. During the last four or five years, the left in Britain has begun to re-assess its conception of politics. Much of this re-assessment has been a product of the electoral failings of 1979 and 1983, but there have been other factors of equal importance. One has been the influence of a variety of social movements on the left (feminists, blacks, ecologists, etc.), whose presence and patterns of organization have demanded an examination of how socialism is to be constituted. Another has been the increased willingness of some writers to question the inalienable 'truths' of the socialist tradition.

This re-assessment has recently produced a predictable backlash against 'revisionism' by Marxist fundamentalists, the terrain for this debate being the question of 'class politics' itself. Given the renewed topicality of this issue, it is appropriate that we should assess the problem of class in the context of that class politics debate.

The revisionism which inspired the debate arose as a product of Gramscian and Italian Eurocommunist influences on the British left during the 1970s. Italian Eurocommunism advocated an incremental socialism built upon policy reforms and the expansion and completion of the process of democracy. Central to this project was the establishment of an 'historic compromise', an alliance between a multiplicity of popular forces which would have the objective of winning governmental power.

The debate around 'popular alliances' has come to the forefront of left debate in Britain and it has been suggested that this is giving rise to a radical re-alignment of the left; on the one side groupings devoted to a British 'historic compromise' of popular forces and movements (Eurocommunists in the Communist Party, the Labour Co-ordinating Committee, sections of the women's movement, etc.); on the other side an alliance of 'the old Trotskyist far left, the Labour Party hard left and sectarians within the Communist Party' which is committed to an alliance against monopoly capital led by the (male) industrial working class (see Campbell, 1984, p. 26: though note Milne, 1984, who rightly qualifies this idea of re-alignment).

What is involved in all of this, however, is not merely the question of re-alignment but the problem of socialist strategy and the very meaning of socialism itself. If advocates of 'popular alliance' are challenging the primacy of class politics, they are obliged to put something in its place to define the socialism to which they aspire. For, as a recent 'fundamentalist' contributor to the debate has rightly said, the working class is, for classical Marxism, not merely the agency of socialist transition but, through its objectively defined interest, the very incarnation of socialism (Meiksins Wood, 1983, pp. 267–8).

Without doubt the most sustained attack on the new revisionism has come from Fine and his associates. In their view the social democratic policies put forward by revisionism — what they term the 'newer left' — are based upon a misapprehension of political reality. The weakness of the British economy, coupled with a period of 'intensifying class struggle', limits the room for manoeuvre available to social democracy (Fine *et al.*, 1984, pp. 21–2, 63). The same point is expressed starkly by two of Fine's associates addressing the problem of British feminism. The same intensifying class struggle, we are told, 'will leave the women's movement high and dry on the shores of bourgeois democracy unless we can once again grasp our revolutionary potential' (Weir and Wilson, 1984, p. 103).

These critics of the 'newer left' are particularly sceptical of the 'new orthodoxy' about Thatcherism, as expressed by writers like Stuart Hall, Andrew Gamble and Eric Hobsbawm. Contrary to the image of Thatcherism as evidence of a 'great moving right show' amongst the British populace, which has transformed the ground rules of politics (Hall, 1979), they suggest that Thatcherism is something of a chimera. Indeed, they rightly claim that there is little empirical or electoral evidence to indicate a profound ideological shift to the right. (It is interesting that the same view is expressed by a recent, non-partisan, critic: 'Marxist commentators have conferred on Thatcherism greater coherence and consistency than it has had in practice'; Riddell, 1983, p. 19.)

However justified their scepticism of certain aspects of the 'newer left', Fine *et al.* fail to present a convincing defence of class politics. Indeed, the most obvious thing about this defence is their lack of consistency about what is meant by 'class'. For example, the working class is defined in three different ways. First, it is equated with a militancy with which the Labour Party, as 'betrayer', is 'out of touch' (Fine *et al.*, 1984, pp. 33; 62−3). Secondly, it is equated with unionized labour as if unionization was an index of class unity (Fine *et al.*, 1984, pp. 24−5). This overlooks several points: that around 40 per cent of unionized labour is now white collar labour (see Hyman, 1984, p. 92); that there are clear differences in political interest between public and private sector employees (see Dunleavy, 1980, ch. 3). Finally, the working class is seen as a means of homogenizing 'popular' movements. For example, despite factors such as discrimination which might set men apart from women in the work process, women are perceived as part of a more or less homogeneous 'wage labour', rather than as 'women wage labourers' (Fine *et al.*, 1984, p. 42).

Despite talking about the relationship of class and non-class issues, then, Fine *et al.* invoke the same totalistic conception of political ideology criticized earlier. It is assumed that because women, blacks, and nuclear disarmers are all 'workers' and 'unionists', their interests will achieve compatibility within an overall class unity. What this argument still fails to address, however, is the problem of the constitution of political interests and the means by which they might become unified. All Fine and his associates have to offer by way of compensation for this absence is a re-assertion of the omnipresence of class unity, there being 'no better example of this [sic] than the miner's strike' (Weir and Wilson, 1984, p. 101).

However platitudinous this defence might be there is a danger that it evokes sympathy amongst socialists because of the emotive appeal of class politics. Some writers, though fully mindful of the sterility of that defence, therefore remain fearful of 'throwing the baby out with the bath-water' (Phillips, 1985, p. 29). Such confusion arises because of what the class politics debate fails to address. The point is not whether class should be 'dropped' from socialist politics or relegated to a secondary status, but whether it is adequate to the demands that socialists have *always* placed on it as a sphere where political interests are encapsulated. The issue is not merely class, but the concept of interests to which socialists are attached.

Some revisionists have rightly challenged traditional Marxist conceptions of class interest and by so doing, have proposed a new socialist pluralism, though as we shall suggest later, some of this pluralism is rather half-hearted. McLennan, for example, advocates a political reality which is pluralistic; one where there are 'a series of different contradictions or sites of struggle'. The existence of such plural sites will imply plural channels of representation (parties, unions, campaigns, clubs and so on) and any overlap between interests 'will largely be the product of the way in which they are worked through politically' (McLennan, 1984, p. 31).

McLennan's argument is carried out against the background of the discussion of 'popular alliances', a conception of politics which, it has been said, is at the core of the new revisionism. Now it is to go against the grain of current left thinking if one suggests that this concept is more the site of a problem for the left than a solution to its difficulties. But certain difficulties are apparent. To begin with, the concept of popular alliance has two different meanings in current left debate. In some instances it refers to more or less narrowly defined electoral pacts geared towards the winning of governmental power; a sort of British 'historic compromise' (see, for instance, Hobsbawm, 1982; for a discussion of the politics of coalition in this context, see Pimlott, 1984). Here, alliance is the pre-condition of an event − a left government. But it is also conceived in a broader sense as part of a continuing transitional process of which electoral victory is only one element and by no means the most important one (Hall, 1984).

This dualism reflects the differences between electoral and Gramscian versions of socialism, a fact borne out by the heated debate in Italian left circles during the 1970s on whether they were compatible. But in some respects this debate obscures a more serious shortcoming of the popular alliance strategy, namely its failure to isolate particular sites of politics, their possibilities and limitations.

The point is well illustrated by current readings of the British political conjuncture. Consider first the state of 'the right'. Advocates of popular alliance derive the need for it not just from successive Labour electoral defeats, but from the 'great moving right' context in which they are allegedly located. Thatcherist hegemony has instituted a form of popular domination or 'authoritarian populism' (Hall, 1980). However, as we have said, evidence for this is questionable. Writers like Hall assume that an electoral change is a sign of some deeper 'structural' change, by virtue of the Gramscian principle of ensemblement. But this ignores the particular qualities of Britain's electoral system, not least its capacity to produce large electoral swings from relatively small changes in voting behaviour. This is not to undermine the real electoral problems facing Labour — one can only be pessimistic about future prospects — but it is to argue that advocates of the new populism are unaware of the particular possibilities and limitations of electoral politics.

Nor is the analysis of left politics any more convincing. Those who advocate more than a narrow electoralism are still wedded to a totalistic conception of socialism. There is, in effect, a contradiction between the pluralism to which they aspire and the totalistic conception of politics and political interests to which they are still attached.

Evidence for this may be found in two examples. First, consider Hall's account of the 'crisis of Labourism'. Hall sees the Labour Party as a necessary component of any popular strategy. Indeed, it has to be the focus of a new hegemony (a sort of 'great moving left show'). In conse-quence, Labour is viewed through the lens of a totalistic politics of hegemony. Hall bemoans the fact that the party has 'become [sic] an electoral rather than a political machine' and that it 'still looks like a party which has never heard of the . . . war of position [sic]' (1984, p. 33). The problem with Labour is its lack of a 'philosophy' and a 'vision' of the future. Indeed, 'what is at stake is no more and no less than "the people"; the popular will' (Hall, 1984, p. 35).

Measured on these evangelistic criteria one would assume that the Labour Party has always been in 'crisis'. But it is not merely that the Labour Party, given its history and organization, is incapable of meeting the sorts of demands that Hall places on it. For there are *no* political constituencies which could provide the means of such a totalistic trans-formation of social relations. The problem is that Hall assumes that socialism can be an adequate vehicle for representing the plural move-ments of the left in an all-encompassing constituency, 'the people'.

Failure to address this problem of 'popular unity' in its wider, extra-electoral, sense is apparent in a second instance, the attempt to invoke 'democracy', 'equality' or 'liberty' as general conditions of unification of the left. This proposition is at the centre of much current left thinking.

It has already been suggested that, in the hands of writers like Laclau and Mouffe, a concept like 'democracy' serves much the same function (as unifier of 'the people') as 'class interest' does (as unifier of the working class). What we have, in effect, is a case of 'different words, same tune'. This is not to suggest that there is anything wrong with 'democracy', merely to point to the function of that term in maintaining a particularly limited conception of politics. (For an indication of the limitations of the concept of 'equality' on socialist social policy, see Rose, 1980.)

What the 'new revisionism' confronts us with, then, is the combination of a radical break with class politics, by virtue of a genuine denial of class primacy, coupled with an incorporation of the same political assumptions which render it problematic. Political interests are still conceived as somehow collapsible into aggregated heaps; democracy *v.* authoritarianism; equality *v.* inequality.

What this view fails to recognize is the constitutive rather than representational nature of political interests. Political interests are constituted in a number of diverse practices; in the identification of objectives; in the ordering of objectives into some form of priority; in the establishment of policies, programmes, organizations, institutions and alliances around given objectives; in the foundation of parties, unions, pressure groups and committees whose objective may be to 'represent' those interests and so on. In this sense, interests are never 'given' prior to the political processes in which they are entangled. In the course of this entanglement, interests may be constructed and reconstructed, objectives amended or abandoned. They are never 'objectively' given to subjects, to be adequately represented in politics.

Two things are suggested by what has been said here. First, political interests and objectives can never be separated from their organizational context. For example, it makes no sense to talk about political organizations as if they were subjects with essential interests and a means of adequately representing them. The Labour Party, for example, is not a subject, but a number of sites of conflict and pressure − conference, NEC, PLP, unions, constituency parties − whose interests may conflict or overlap according to circumstances (cf. Pimlott, 1984, p. 205). Secondly, political interests cannot be reduced to a distillation of some essential political or moral objective. This is not an argument against moral objectives, merely an affirmation of the fact that moral objectives are converted into specific political forms by the practices of political organizations. Democracy is not merely a moral objective, it is also a variety of political mechanisms. That is why Thatcherism can, like the left, lay claim to be the authentic means of representation of democracy. But the adequate representation of a moral principle cannot be invoked as a means of 'uniting the people', any more than it can be cited as the means of uniting a class.

This means that there is a contradiction between the pluralism advocated by some revisionists and the conception of politics to which they are still attached. McLennan's recognition of the diversity of interests has to lead to a more radical re-appraisal of socialism than revisionists are, so far, willing to make. There is no necessary reason to assume, for example, that the plural sites of struggle comprising 'the left' will cohere into something called 'socialism' at all.

The demand for a pluralistic socialism, therefore, has far-reaching implications. For one thing, it is incompatible with holistic conceptions of society where politics is seen as a process of conflict between relatively unified forces. Again, this is not an argument against unity, but an insistence that unity is specific to given objectives and political constituencies. The left's continued pre-occupation with the search for a universalistic and homogeneous socialism (once embodied in classes, now increasingly embodied in 'the people') has to be abandoned. That form of socialism does not exist and never will.

We shall return to the question of socialist pluralism later. There also, a final comment will be made about the concept of class, though it should be obvious by now that the argument has moved beyond 'class' to a wider consideration of the conception of politics which the left invokes. For the moment, however, let us reconsider another theme, central to the argument, that of economic and social agency.

Economic and social agency: the enterprise

It has been suggested in Chapter 3 that Marxist critics of managerialism have conducted their arguments on the terrain of managerialists, a consequence of the inability of both discourses to recognize the effects of legal conditions on the constitution of economic agents. Typically, the left has viewed the enterprise as an institution dominated by a group of powerful shareholders. According to this view the corporation cannot be a 'real' agent in its own right because possession has to reside in 'real social groups' (see Scott, 1979, pp. 32–5).

However, the suggestion of Chapter 3, that legal relations can be effective in constituting non-subjective entities (corporations) as economic agents, provides the basis for a conception of social agency quite different from that adopted by both sociological and Marxist traditions. Indeed, in the case of the enterprise, it has been suggested, not only that it is an agent in its own right, but that it is effective in shaping the economic agents located therein: 'The firm largely constructs the agents and sub agencies operating within it and the patterns of practices and procedures that they operate there' (Thompson, 1982, p. 242).

But are all of these agents not ultimately reducible, as writers like Scott would maintain, to individual human subjects? After all, is it not transparently 'obvious' that action and decision-making are a function of individual actors?

It is suggested here that this question of agency is neither obvious nor transparent. On the contrary, there may be a variety of social conditions (law, organizational structure, cultural habituation) that affect the constitution of social agents. For example, it is possible to find many cases of social relations where *only* non-individual agents can function as legitimate agents of action. Take the case of trades unions as agents of economic action. Unions are the agents which undertake the responsibility of contractual bargaining on behalf of their members. The individual member may be required, for the purposes of employment, to sign a wage labour contract, but the terms of that contract are not determined, nor even usually influenced, by the individual. The union's prior decisions as agent of economic action bind the wage labourer to certain contractual terms. The member has no authority or status to undertake separate contractual bargaining with the employer. In this particular sphere, then, the individual has no legal or customary status as agent.

It could still, of course, be argued that the actions or decisions of the union are merely a function of the aggregated actions or decisions of its individual members. But the processes of decision-making are never so reducible, precisely because decision-making is always subject to the effects of specific organizational conditions of existence. To take one simple example, it is evident that the process of arriving at a 'collective' decision by a union is dependent, not only on the availability of information and the manner of its distribution, but also on processes such as voting. In the case of voting, it is apparent that the manner in which votes are cast and enumerated has quite specific effects on the nature of decisions reached. The internal processes of calculating and weighing votes in unions, business corporations and political parties (card votes, proportional representation, or whatever) have an effect which makes the reduction of collective decisions to the actions of individuals impossible. In short, the effects of the conditions of existence of social action ensure that social relations cannot be ultimately reduced to the allegedly essential capacities of individual human subjects.

Having raised the question of economic agency, a second matter which deserves comment concerns the problem of 'control', for it is undoubtedly the case that both managerialists and their socialist critics have conceived the problem of the corporation as a problem of 'who controls'? Once one questions the necessary equation of agent and individual subject, however, the claims made by managerialists and their critics about the nature and capacities of managerial agents of 'control' are called into doubt. The 'soulfulness' of managers does not prove the demise of capitalist private property any more than their desire for profit maximization establishes them as 'capital personified'.

Tomlinson has rightly suggested that an adequate socialist theory of corporate enterprise has to re-think its approach to the problem of control. Traditionally, both managerialists and socialists have regarded control as an activity of certain categories of subjects who are representative of given interests. Corporate practices are, in effect, always seen to represent something which is situated outside the corporation ('capitalism', 'the public consensus', etc.) through the mediation of a constitutive subject. The corporation is effectively seen as the site of power struggles whose essence lies elsewhere (Tomlinson, 1982, pp. 93–6).

Tomlinson makes two important suggestions. First, he argues that socialists need to give serious consideration to the problem of 'what controls?' rather than 'who controls?' corporate enterprise. Little attention has been paid, for example, to the effects of financial institutions on corporate practice and where such institutions have been examined, socialists have tried to reduce their practices to the capacities of constitutive subjects. Secondly, it is suggested that 'control' can no longer be regarded as an attribute or capacity of subjects, but should be conceived as a 'series of practices'. Two things are implied in this argument. First, control should no longer be theorized as an essentially *subjective* capacity. Secondly, it should no longer be conceived as a *capacity* at all, but as a series of practices pertaining to different sites, within and outside the enterprise, which can give rise to variable outcomes. According to this view the enterprise should not be theorized as a subject, secure in its capacity to control its own destiny, but as a site of struggles for such control.

A similar notion is implied in Thompson's conception of the firm as a 'dispersed social agency' (1982, p. 235). Rather than seeing the firm as a unity, controlled by a subject, able to realize its objectives ('management'), Thompson argues that managerial objectives will always be subject to obstacles and constraints. This does not mean that all loci of decision-making are equal in strength. But it does mean that the possessing agent never enjoys an unproblematic 'control' of the enterprise.

The implications of Thompson's and Tomlinson's arguments are two-fold. First, there can be no 'general' theory of the enterprise, since there is no single homogeneous entity called 'the enterprise'. Secondly, the enterprise is not a unity, but a set of diverse practices, the importance of which will vary according to particular objectives. In other words, having calculated political objectives, socialists will focus on particular practices at particular times. The object 'the enterprise' will, therefore, be conditioned by the particular objective in question – output, level of employment, or whatever (see Tomlinson, 1982, p. 124).

If the enterprise is conceived as a 'locus of decision-making', what, then, of 'ownership and control'? So far it has been argued that once the legal conditions of possession are deemed effective, the 'separation' (dissolution of the 'unity of property') advocated by managerialists and partly conceded by Marxists is impossible to sustain. But what is the effect on this argument of conceiving the issue of 'control' in a sense incompatible with that of managerialists and Marxists alike? Can property continue to be conceived in a unitary sense?

The answer to this question is almost certainly in the negative. Legal conditions may be effective in the constitution of agents, but there is no reason to assume the effects of these conditions to be uniform:

> the obligations and responsibilities placed on . . . legal statuses and the right accorded to them vary considerably . . . there are considerable differences between the forms of incorporation and the types of obligations that this imparts upon . . . agents. (Thompson, 1982, p. 245)

Legal conditions, then, neither guarantee 'control' of the means of production, nor do they impose uniform rights and obligations. This is confirmed in a recent paper which examines the case of pension funds. This example shows that ownership is 'a complex notion which can assume different forms in different contexts'. Here we are confronted by a financial institution which 'is both object and agent: it owns and is owned, controls and is controlled' (Schuller and Hyman, 1984, p. 67).

What these arguments would suggest is that the category 'ownership/control' is incapable of conveying the complex relations which may exist in an enterprise or institution. Property is not unitary, and possession/separation cannot be conceived in the 'all or nothing' sense advocated by Marxists and managerialists alike through the problematic of ownership and control. A socialist strategy towards the enterprise has to begin from a recognition of the complexity of those relations.

There are certain obvious implications which such a 'particularistic' view of the enterprise might have for socialist strategy. For example, the left has had a peculiarly ambivalent attitude towards the law. On the one hand, it has regarded it as illusory and ineffectual. On the other hand, it has had a strangely naive respect for its potential through the policy of nationalization, which assumes 'that the legal status of property is a crucial determinant of the organization and use of that property' (Tomlinson, 1982, p. 64). If one argues that the law has specific rather than general effects, however, socialists may legitimately argue for progressive legal reforms of a particular nature. This, in turn, suggests that traditional left slogans of 'worker control', 'democracy', 'nationalization' and the like, are at worst inadequate and at best in need of specification.

An example of what might be considered here is the question of enterprise size as a factor in 'worker control' (see Tomlinson, 1982, p. 18). As we have seen in Chapter 3, Marxism has conceived the problem of the enterprise according to the teleology of monopoly capitalism. Size is considered progressive because it is indicative of the socialization of the productive forces (e.g. Marx's 'co-operative factory'). In the absence of teleology, however, and recognizing the non-uniform effects of law, the possibility of progressive legal reforms (smaller enterprises, specific forms of worker control) may be placed on the agenda.

The state and socialist political intervention

The approach to the enterprise described above relates closely to the conception of the state that is proposed here. For example, the state cannot be said to have an essential function, be it repressive or ideological domination. Nor can it be regarded as synonymous with 'politics'. Questions of political conflict, power and ideology are central to all institutions be they formal state apparatuses or not. The state cannot be encapsulated as a 'political' component of the totality of forms. Furthermore, from what has been said it is clear that the state cannot be considered as an adequate means of representation of a given set of interests ('the nation', 'the ruling class', 'the proletariat'). Rather than conceiving the state as a relatively unitary 'structure', then, it has, for the purposes of socialist political intervention, to be 'de-constructed' and the 'specificity' of its practices and institutions considered in relation to political issues and objectives. Let us consider for a moment what this might imply in broad terms.

First, it has been suggested that power is a relation not a capacity and, as such, may be constituted within various sites. If the state is conceived in this sense, it is no longer a subject which 'exercises' power, but a location – or more accurately a set of locations – where conflicts occur.

Secondly, it follows that the concept of 'state' has to give way to that of 'state apparatuses'. The relationship between state apparatuses then becomes a political problem. This does not mean that there is no co-ordination between branches of 'the state', only that such co-ordination may be problematic. Indeed, in some cases the lack of cohesion between state apparatuses can offer potential for exploitation by social and political forces.

Instances of 'non-cohesion' between state institutions are not difficult to identify. Consider, for example, the way in which Conservative education cuts have been implemented since 1979. DES policy has been geared towards inflicting more stringent restrictions on humanities and social sciences than on science and technology. In fact, that policy has failed to have the intended consequences:

> figures show that Government policy has been less than successful in shifting the balance between arts and science subjects . . . in spite of Government attempts to switch the emphasis of higher education towards science and technology, this year will see a fall in the number of engineering and technology students graduating. (O'Connor, 1985)

To understand this disparity one has, amongst other things, to consider conflicts of interest within and between decision-making bodies in 'the state' (for example, the University Grants Committee has, in the past, been dominated by humanities rather than scientific interests). Alternatively, one might consider the peculiar relationship that existed between the Home Office and the Community Development Projects between 1968 and 1978. Here, a department of state first legitimized and then funded a programme of research which increasingly took on the form of an overt challenge to state policy, without ever exerting serious organizational control over planning or content (see Loney, 1983). Such examples, in themselves, are not important. What is crucial is the realization that state apparatuses and institutions cannot be assumed to have a uniform character and a common function.

Thirdly, different objectives and issues deemed to be matters for socialist concern will require an analysis of different sites of conflict within the state and between state apparatuses and other sectors of society. There will, for example, be a variety of state processes (financial, cultural, organizational, legal) which impinge on issues in varying ways and to varying degrees. There is no simple and universal 'state effect' on issues and an understanding of the variability of effects is crucial to a socialist analysis.

What, then, of socialist political intervention relating to particular state apparatuses? Let us consider a single issue in some detail, the question of policing and democratic accountability, a topical debate amongst socialist writers and one which raises questions both about state apparatuses and democracy in socialist politics.

Before commencing, three things need to be emphasized. First, this is not intended as an adequate discussion of socialist policing strategy, merely an indication of some of the issues which are at stake, given the arguments presented here. Secondly, the consideration of this issue is not intended to imply some general socialist strategy towards state apparatuses. The approach to state apparatuses presented here suggests that there may be different political conditions affecting different institutions and apparatuses which preclude such generalization. Thirdly, the fact that socialist politics is being considered in relation to 'the state' does not imply that strategies directed there have priority over those aimed at non-state institutions.

Left debates on democratizing the police have inevitably centred on questions of 'community policing' in recent years. It is possible to distinguish three broad approaches to this question:

(1) *Rejection* (e.g. Gordon, 1984). Since the state functions as a vehicle of domination, the function of community policing is one of social control. Community policing is the 'velvet glove' attached to the 'iron fist' of 'reactive policing'. The community police officer is at the centre of a web of inter-agency information gathering. Community policing 'hives off'

the crime prevention aspect of policing to the public ('neighbourhood watches', etc.), leaving the police to concentrate on the increasing problem of public order.

(2) *Strategic support* (e.g. Savage, 1984). Community liaison schemes potentially offer more effective accountability than direct demands for political control of the police through elected bodies. The latter approach, exemplified by the Straw Bills of 1979 and 1980, raise serious difficulties that the left has failed to resolve. First, the 'general' policing matters, to be subjected to political control, are effectively inseparable from 'day to day' policing matters. Secondly, demands for 'accountability' side-step the problem of what a left police authority would 'do' once in office. In fact, Savage doubts whether policing can be subject to a political 'policy' in the same way as education or planning, as it involves the full constituency of law. Thirdly, and most seriously, demands for control of the apparatus fail to appreciate the extent of discretion enjoyed by police constables. Community liaison is, therefore, more suited to representing community interests at the level of practical policing. Savage accepts that the potential of liaison is likely to be affected by other factors however, such as the way in which schemes are organized and the way committees are constituted.

(3) *Limited strategic support* (e.g. Lea and Young, 1984). Community policing and its related consultative machinery are not equivalent to real 'democratic police accountability'. The latter involves the local community deciding policy rather than being 'consulted'. Socialists should seek a genuinely representative form of local control — since, otherwise, direction by a left police authority would be no better than by a chief constable. 'Consultation' on the democratic model suggests that the community consults the police, not vice versa. A rigorously qualified support should be given to liaison schemes. Borough police committees should use liaison to enable representatives on liaison schemes to present a cohesive set of demands to the police. The clearer community demands, the more police refusal to accede to them will demonstrate the need for real democratic control.

Gordon's view that policing serves an essentially repressive function is, like all essentialist theories of state apparatuses, unacceptable. His comment that community policing represents the 'soft' and penetrative side of repression has, of course, to be considered as a possible 'future' none the less. The point is, however, that its possibility is dependent upon a variety of political conditions — not least the left's own political interventions — which essentialism cannot recognize. It is quite right for authors like Gordon to insist that community policing cannot be divorced from 'reactive' policing, but it does not follow that the two are elements of a totality with no space for political manoeuvre between them. It is precisely because there is such a space within a police apparatus that cannot be conceived as merely homogeneous and unified, that left intervention in policing policy may be possible. There is a political conflict to be fought over policing whose outcome is not pre-determined by some essential unity of purpose enjoyed by the state.

To propose such a view requires one neither to be over-optimistic nor politically naive. On the contrary, there are developments in policing and criminal justice of which the left are justifiably wary (the Police and Criminal Evidence Bill; demands by certain chief constables for further concentration of police forces; fears that the National Reporting Centre constitutes a de facto 'nationalization' of policing). Yet even the miner's strike — which gave those advocating police reform few grounds for optimism — has shown marked variations between the policing strategies of different forces. (Witness not merely Gerald Kaufmann's commendation of Devon and Cornwall Constabulary, but media and community reports of the varying police responses of neighbouring forces in Yorkshire). In this sense, it is equally 'naive' for the left to ignore such variations by regarding them as subsumable within an overall network of social control.

If we regard such variations in the police apparatus as real and if we consider community policing to provide some space, however limited, for left intervention, the crucial question posed for socialists concerns how community policing relates, both to 'reactive' forms of policing and to the organization of policing at national and local levels.

It is not just that socialists have to address this issue. The crucial question is how they address it. One thing which Savage's argument points to is that left demands for 'democratic control' of policing have had a tendency to ignore the conditional nature of such control. For example, it would be naive to assume that the formality of legal control by a democratically elected police authority would necessarily achieve control of the behaviour of police officers. This is not to under-estimate the importance of law, merely to point to its conditional nature. The problem is well illustrated by the case of complaints procedure. It is one thing to establish a formally just and independent complaints procedure. It is quite another to make it work (cf. the comment made by Smith in his analysis of the Metropolitan Police: 'we believe that police officers will normally tell lies to prevent another officer from being disciplined or prosecuted, and this is the belief of senior officers who handle complaints and discipline cases' 1983, p. 329).

'Control' and 'democratic accountability' are, therefore, always conditional. They are, moreover, conditioned by a multiplicity of factors. As Baldwin and Kinsey (1982, pp. 284—5) emphasize, it is imperative that those seeking reform recognize the multiple sites of political intervention which must be confronted before any realistic effect on policing strategy can be achieved. For example, legal reform alone cannot guarantee effective change within an organization of the police's size and complexity. To achieve a consensual policing whose focus is on the local community, a wide range of reforms will be necessary; a reduction in the size of police bureaucracies or, if that is not realistic, a devolution of power within the present system to give autonomy at divisional and subdivisional levels for responding to community demands; a re-evaluation of the job status of beat officers and the allocation of personnel to community policing in sufficient numbers to give it more than 'Cinderella' status; more sensitive training procedures and so on. If organizational aspects of reform are not confronted, then legal changes will have little effect. But equally, it may be necessary to back up such reforms with further legal changes. For example, if community policing is to be more than information gathering, it may, as Alderson himself has suggested, be necessary to have a bill of rights as one of its attendant conditions (1982, p. 11).

Community policing may, then, offer some scope for political intervention by the left, but in so doing it raises problems which require serious consideration. Perhaps the most important of these concerns the question of the 'democracy' upon which demands for democratic accountability and control are constructed. So far, demands for democratic control have been doubly problematic. In the first place, control has been conceived in a non-conditional sense. In the second place, 'democracy' has been seen — in accordance with the classical socialist conception of politics — as the adequate means of representation of a moral end or political interest. It is suggested here, however, that democracy has to be seen as a political mechanism which is neither uniform in structure nor in consequent effects.

It is interesting that some socialist writers on policing recognize that democracy cannot be a guarantor of its own ends. Both Jefferson and Grimshaw (1982, p. 98) and Lea and Young imagine the situation where a democratically elected police authority either fails to follow majority opinion, or fails to protect specific minority groups: 'One of our constant nightmares is that if there was a completely democratic control of police in areas such as Hackney, the resulting police force would look exactly the same as the present Hackney police force' (Lea and Young, 1984, p. 270).

There are two problems here. First, there is the question of the 'community' to be represented. Here, the representing agent can never be adequate to the varying and often conflicting interests that exist in a locality. Whether 'democratically elected' or not, that agent will still face charges of partiality and discrimination, since no democratic mechanism in a pluralistic context can guarantee 'fairness'. As Lea and Young rightly say 'locally controlled policing would be unlikely to produce a consensual policy acceptable to all social and ethnic groups living in an area' (1984, p. 238). Second, there is the question of the constituent bodies that represent the community. Savage points to the problematic status of political parties as a means of representation of community interests in a policing context (1984, p. 58). A similar point is made by Lea and Young who, pointing to the wholesale political marginalization of ethnic and youth populations in the city, pose the problem of 'who the representatives actually represent' (1984, p. 248).

The solution to this sort of problem — recognizing that any solution is partial — would appear to be precisely those plural forms of representation referred to by writers like McLennan. The point is, however, that to invoke 'democratic control' is to raise a number of complex and *enduring* problems. 'Democracy' is not, in itself, a solution to political issues as much socialist debate appears currently to imply, for a democratic mechanism, if one may be excused the pun, has no 'end'. Democracy is a mechanism, not merely an abstract moral postulate. As such, its processes, like those of any other decision-making mechanism, are conditioned by the particular forms that mechanism takes (e.g. rules on voting practices or those which define electoral boundaries), by the particular agents which operate that mechanism and by the constituencies that mechanism aims to represent.

Now in the case of this final point it is clear that there are serious difficulties regarding the constituency which is to be democratically represented under a locally accountable police force. It is significant that Alderson sees community policing, not merely as a means of representing communities, but as a means of constituting them through police leadership (see Baldwin and Kinsey, 1982, p. 229). Even if socialists refute this elitism, some would accept the problem he identifies. Lea and Young, for example, argue that political marginalization has the effect of destroying the community. Rather than waiting for the community to 'emerge' as a politically responsible body seeking representation, they insist that the community has to be constructed. The only way of doing this is for the left 'to create the institutions of local democracy' (Lea and Young, 1984, p. 239) and thereby re-constitute the community as a political entity.

If one accepts this position as a starting point for a socialist policing policy — and indeed for other areas of policy — there are, however, two questions which follow from it. First, what mechanisms and bodies will comprise the means of democratic representation in the sphere of policing? That, it must be said, is a political question not merely a technical one. Mechanisms of representation, after all, always have effects on the constituencies to be represented. Secondly, what principles, objectives and mechanisms would provide the basis for such institutions to adjudicate between competing interests when they arise? The point here is that the concept of 'community' cannot be allowed to gloss over the effects of plural interests in the way that 'class interest' has in other contexts. Socialists cannot invoke community as a means of abstaining on the problem of choice between different constituencies and their interests. So far, in debates on policing, as in other areas of left debate, it has to be said that concepts like 'community' and 'democracy' have been used, with rare exceptions, in this way. But if socialist pluralism is to take its pluralism seriously, it cannot avoid political choices of this sort.

On socialist pluralism

The analysis presented in this book is supportive of a socialist pluralism which takes account of three things. First, the existence of varied social forces with potentially diverse interests, some more and some less amenable to socialist politics. Secondly, the recognition of plural sites of conflict in society, none of which can be ontologically prioritized for socialism. Thirdly, the need for socialists to recognize that, in consequence, varied strategies of political intervention may be demanded to achieve socialist objectives.

But what of these objectives? It has been maintained here that there is no essential constituency of interests or objectives that can be deemed socialist. This view might seem objectionable to some. For instance, there are those who might want to found socialism on an ethic such as 'equality'. The problem is, however, that when one confronts socialist politics, one finds a variability of political forms emanating from that ethic. Socialists, in pursuing equality, have advocated common owner-ship of the means of production, the re-distribution of income and wealth, universal social welfare provision, dictatorship of the proletariat, popular democratic forms of political representation and so on. In effect, the example merely serves to confirm the variable content of socialist objectives. To invoke equality is to tell us very little about the forms of politics which might comprise socialism.

The suggestion that there is no essential constituency to socialist politics also contrasts with the Marxist view. Here, ontological and teleological principles of determination provide the means of deriving an essential socialist politics from the structure of capitalist reality: socialist transition is conceivable only in its lawful derivation from the capitalist mode of production; socialism is inscribed within the class interests of an essential agent, the proletariat. And we have seen that even those 'non-reductionist' Marxisms which reach beyond mere 'class politics' still read political interests in the same essentialist form as the reductionism they criticize.

It is suggested here, however, that once one refuses to conceive social relations in the form of a totality, that combination of ontology/teleology and the view of politics it sustains cannot be maintained. If socialists choose to give priority to the problem of transforming capitalist economic relations, this is not because the economy determines the structure of the social totality — in the last, or any other instance. In the absence of totality, there is no obligation to invoke essential forces and agents to explain the processes of social relations, since those social relations have no essential function or future direction. Socialist priorities and objectives do not reflect the ontological structure of reality. They are a product of political objectives and political ideologies. They have no essential structure, defined outside the processes of political ideology and calculation.

It has been emphasized here, then, that the content of socialist ideology is contestable and, moreover, has to be contested. The problem with the Marxist tradition is that it stifles any such initiative by sanctioning practices of theoretical foreclosure. *That is why, it must be emphasized once again, Marxism is rejected not for its 'reductionism', but for the politically limiting effects of its theoretical problematic.* The purpose of this book has been to challenge that problematic and open up socialist ideology to critical examination, the results of which cannot be pre-determined by theory. This is not a rejection of theory. On the contrary, it is maintained that a rigorous socialist theory is the pre-condition of any effective socialist politics. What is rejected, however, is the possibility of a general socialist theory which can be 'applied' to varied political problems and conditions. A rigorous socialist theory has to be one directed at specific objectives and possibilities.

As this work has been a theoretical critique of one predominant form of socialist analysis, it has not been concerned with the problem of discussing socialist objectives and policies. Indeed, the rationale has been that such objectives and policies would require the writing of a different book; a book directed at the possibilities and limitations of socialist intervention in appropriately defined areas of politics; at how these areas might be articulated with one another, and so on.

Having said that, let us return briefly to the question of objectives. It has already been said that socialist objectives can only be defined in terms of what has been referred to elsewhere as 'discursive priority' (Cutler *et al.*, 1977). In the light of this, let us consider one definition of socialist objectives which, we believe, provides a suitable starting point for discussion:

> Socialists are concerned to displace commodity and bureaucratic forms of production and distribution through the development of non-commodity forms subject to popular democratic control. (Hindess, 1981, p. 29).

By way of conclusion, let us now assess this definition in relation to some of the comments made here.

In Britain, socialism is set in a varied political context. For one thing there are diverse agents, forces, movements and interests (parties pressure groups, single issue organizations, voters, state apparatuses, business enterprises, unions, ethnic groups, etc.). For another, the political conditions which surround such diversity are by no means uniform. Stable parliamentary traditions, and a long established system of electoral politics, co-exist with various forms of extra-parliamentary activity (strikes, demonstrations, the movements of international money markets and their effects), with a multiplicity of political organizations and groups (some more and some less amenable to socialist politics) and with a substantial degree of political marginalization amongst particular social groups (blacks, the young, the unemployed).

This political context has marked effects on socialist objectives. *The definition of such objectives, after all, tells us relatively little about the forms of politics which emanate from them.* It is not merely that particular socialisms, in different political contexts, seek to achieve sometimes similar objectives differently. That much has already been established. The point is that a statement of socialist objectives cannot be 'binding' on forms of socialist political practice in any clear sense. For example, socialism is inevitably 'particularized' by its context, through the production of policies and programmes. Towards this end, it will inevitably adopt policies in spheres other than 'production' and 'distribution'. Some of these may, so to speak, 'follow' from basic objectives. For instance, socialists might seek to reform non-economic relations which provide conditions of existence of capitalist relations of production and distribution (e.g. the reform of company, trade union or tax law). Others will not conform in this way, however. For example, given the existence of various popular social movements — which may or may not have an interest in socialist objectives — some of which also advocate 'popular democratic control' of certain institutions, it is possible that socialists may seek alliances. But such alliances can neither be conceived as general nor unconditional. For, in this context, they are likely to be directed at some particular objective; an electoral victory at local or national level; the application of pressure on Parliament to institute or amend a specific piece of legislation; the prevention of a hospital or factory closure, etc.

There is an obvious problem here for socialism, as the popular forces with which it allies for the furtherance of common political ends need have no necessary socialist sympathies. Nor, as we have seen, can potential conflicts and differences of interest be overridden by the concept of 'democracy' itself. It cannot be assumed, as we have said, that socialism is an adequate unifier of diverse political forces. Indeed, it cannot even be assumed that socialism enjoys the security of its own unity. Take, for example, the strategy of 'democratization of the workplace'. It is by no means obvious that such an objective is, of itself, compatible with other objectives deemed socialist. For one thing, it might conflict with an objective such as 'inter-enterprise equality' (see Tomlinson, 1982, p.

135). For another, it might, if contained within a movement aimed at the decentralization of economic decision-making, clash with wider objectives of economic planning (see Jones, 1980, p. 150).

There is, then, a problem of how socialism can articulate different sites of conflict, different political forces and different policies. The idea that this problem can be resolved by a general 'unity' (cf. 'popular hegemony') is, however, unacceptable. The real problem for socialism is not general unity but the conditions of establishing compatibility between different policies and objectives and the agents associated with them. This is not merely an emphasis on the particularity rather than the generality of politics, for it implies a very different conception of socialism from the conventional one. For one thing, it involves socialists in making choices and establishing priorities between different policies and objectives. It may involve them in making concessions, either short or long term, to other popular forces. In the case of electoral strategies, for instance, socialists may need to be supportive of policies whose ends are not functional to stated socialist objectives. There can be no general theoretical adjudication on matters of this sort. The problem of articulating plural interests in order to best achieve desired socialist objectives is a problem that can only be confronted politically. For another thing, this eradicates all totalistic and universalistic conceptions of socialism. Socialism is not a homogeneous force which can reconcile all popular objectives and interests. All it can aim to do is to establish sufficient cohesion in order for it to produce the political conditions (electoral or other) by which objectives may be achieved.

This suggests two things. First, different conditions will place different limitations on political objectives and may necessitate varying strategic responses. Failure to recognize this can lead to serious difficulties. Labour Party policy on housing, for example, seems to have been shaped by the same universalistic rhetoric as its policies on education or health. Whereas in health and education universalism was a reality, or near reality, in housing there has always been a substantial private ownership. Universal public provision was, therefore, invoked under political conditions which could not support it. Labour's failure to grasp this nettle led to a policy of 'sitting on the fence'; rhetorical pieties about universal provision were combined with the cynical 'equality between tenures' of the 1977 Green Paper. It has been suggested by some writers that the consequence of this political inertia was Labour's loss of the 'housing issue' to the Conservatives (see Griffiths, 1982; Griffiths, 1984; Griffiths and Holmes, 1984). Significantly, at the time of writing, there appear to be indications that Labour's past policy on council house sales will give way to an acceptance of the principle of 'right to buy', contrary to the line adopted in the 1983 election manifesto.

A second consequence follows from the denial of universalism and the insistence that socialism recognizes the limitations placed on it by varying political conditions. For it cannot be assumed that such objectives as 'popular democratic control', if realized, will be achieved simultaneously across different apparatuses and institutions. Whether progressive changes can be achieved with sufficient simultaneity to constitute what socialists have regarded as a qualitative social transition is something that cannot be predicted.

And finally, what of class in socialist discourse? In this book we have argued for a political analysis which focuses on social relations and their conditions of existence. In order to construct socialist policies towards business enterprises or state apparatuses, one needs an understanding of the legal, economic, organizational, cultural and ideological context in which they are contained. An understanding of the connections between particular sets of social relations and their conditions of existence cannot, however, be conceived according to any totalistic principle. That is why the assumption of a general determination or relative determination of social relations is rejected.

Now, in view of this, it is clear why the concept of class has been considered here to be problematic, since it is contained within precisely such a discourse of general determination. That is why it was suggested in Chapter 7 that the retention of class by Cutler *et al.* was at odds with their attempt to pose the problem of social relations and their conditions of existence. Is it possible, then, to conceptualize class relations (and thus class agency) in a way which is compatible with this project?

An affirmative answer to this question can be given if one advocates 'discursive primacy'. Here, economic class is defined purely in terms of possession/separation, this distinction defining the 'problem' of socialist politics *as* economic class relations, but making no claim that such relations determine the structure of politics (see Cutler *et al.*, 1977, ch. 9; for a rather different version see Cottrell, 1984).

There can be no objection to class being used in this sense, though it is not clear that such a retention has very much purpose. For here, if one is unequivocal about it, 'class' is no more than an allegory of possession/separation. It is of little importance whether socialists retain the concept of class in this sense. What is significant is how they conceive the possession and separation which 'class' signifies. It should be clear, for example, that a class allegory can tell us nothing about the relatively complex variations in possession and separation referred to above, though an understanding of such variations is central to socialist politics.

To suggest that the question of class is of superficial relevance to these matters is not to argue that it is politically insignificant. No reservations that we express about the utility of the *concept* of class in socialist debate can alter the fact that a variety of class *images* have effects on politics.

Such class images may bear a close relationship to classes defined in an economic sense of possession and separation, or the relationship may be very marginal, as when classes are defined in cultural or status terms. But whatever the inadequacies of class in socialist political calculation, the fact remains that political parties and organizations on the left continue to read politics in a variety of class-representational terms. In that sense, class continues to have definite effects on popular politics and a consideration of those effects is, of course, a legitimate concern of socialist theory, though it has not been the concern of this book (cf. Cottrell, 1984).

What should be clear from what has been said, however, is that the crucial issue for socialist concern is not the concept of class itself, but the conception of politics and political interests which the concept has supported. Our examination of Marxist revisionism has shown that a rejection of the primacy of class politics, such as many revisionists advocate, is perfectly compatible with a retention of the same limited conception of politics and political interests that Marxists have always adopted. It is for that reason that we suggest a genuine socialist pluralism requires a far more radical re-appraisal of traditional assumptions than many on the left are yet willing to make.

Bibliography

Alderson, J. (1982), 'Policing in the eighties', *Marxism Today*, April, pp. 9−14.

Allen, V. (1977), 'The differentiation of the working class', in *Class and Class Structure*, ed. A. Hunt (London: Lawrence & Wishart), pp. 61−80.

Althusser, L. (1969), *For Marx* (Harmondsworth: Penguin).

Althusser, L. (1971), *Lenin and Philosophy and Other Essays* (London: New Left Books).

Althusser, L., and Balibar, E. (1975), *Reading Capital* (London: New Left Books).

Altvater, E. (1973), 'Notes on some problems of state intervention', *Kapitalistate*, 1, pp. 96−108 and 2, pp. 76−83.

Anderson, C. H. (1974), *The Political Economy of Social Class* (Englewood Cliffs, New Jersey: Prentice Hall).

Anderson, P. (1967), 'The limits and possibilities of trade union action', in *The Incompatibles*, ed. R. Blackburn and A. Cockburn (Harmondsworth: Penguin), pp. 263−80.

Baldwin, R., and Kinsey, R. (1982), *Police Powers and Politics* (London: Quartet Books).

Balibar, E. (1977), *On the Dictatorship of the Proletariat* (London: New Left Books).

Baran, P., and Sweezy, P. M. (1968), *Monopoly Capital* (Harmondsworth: Penguin).

Becker, J. F. (1973−4), 'Class structure and conflict in the managerial phase', *Science and Society*, Vol. 37, no. 3, pp. 259−77 and no. 4, pp. 437−53.

Berle, A. A. (1960), *Power Without Property* (London: Sidgwick & Jackson).

Berle, A. A., and Means, G. C. (1935), *The Modern Corporation and Private Property* (New York: Macmillan).

Bettelheim, C. (1976), *Economic Calculation and Forms of Property* (London: Routledge & Kegan Paul).

Beynon, H. (1973), *Working for Ford* (Harmondsworth: Penguin).

Blackburn, R. (1967), 'The unequal society', in *The Incompatibles*, ed. R. Blackburn and C. Cockburn (Harmondsworth: Penguin), pp. 15−55.

Blackburn, R. (1972), 'The new capitalism', in *Ideology in Social Science*, ed. R. Blackburn (London: Fontana), pp. 164−86.

Boggs, C. (1976), *Gramsci's Marxism* (London: Pluto).

Bottomore, T., and Rubel, M. (1963), *Karl Marx, Selected Writings in Sociology and Social Philosophy* (Harmondsworth: Penguin).

Braverman, H. (1974), *Labour and Monopoly Capital* (New York: Monthly Review Press).

Buci-Glucksmann, C. (1980), *Gramsci and the State* (London: Lawrence & Wishart).

Burnham, J. (1945), *The Managerial Revolution* (Harmondsworth: Penguin).

Campbell, B. (1984), 'Politics, pyramids and people', *Marxism Today*, December, pp. 22−7.

Carchedi, G. (1977), *On the Economic Identification of Social Classes* (London: Routledge & Kegan Paul).

Child, J. (1969), *The Business Enterprise in Modern Industrial Society* (London: Collier Macmillan).

Clarke, S. (1980), 'Althusserian Marxism', in *One Dimensional Marxism*, by Clarke, S., Seidler, V. J., McDonnell, K., Robins, K., and Lovell, T. (London: Allison & Busby), pp. 7–102.

Colletti, L. (1972), *From Rousseau to Lenin* (London: New Left Books).

Communist Party of Great Britain (1978), *The British Road to Socialism* (London: CPGB).

Cottrell, A. (1984), *Social Classes in Marxist Theory* (London: Routledge & Kegan Paul).

Cutler, A., Hindess, B., Hirst, P., and Hussain, A., (1977–78), *Marx's Capital and Capitalism Today*, Vols. 1 and 2, (London: Routledge & Kegan Paul).

Dahrendorf, R. (1959), *Class and Class Conflict in an Industrial Society* (London: Routledge & Kegan Paul)

De Vroey, M. (1975), 'The separation of ownership and control in large corporations', *Review of Radical Political Economics*, Vol. 7, no. 2, pp. 1–10.

Draper, H. (1977), *Karl Marx's Theory of Revolution* (New York: Monthly Review Press).

Dunleavy, P. (1980), *Urban Political Analysis* (London: Macmillan).

Engels, F. (1876–8), *Anti-Duhring* (London: Lawrence & Wishart, 1975).

Engels, F. (1880), 'Socialism, utopian and scientific', in *Selected Works of Marx and Engels*, one volume edn (London: Lawrence & Wishart, 1968), pp. 375–428.

Engels, F. (1884), 'The origin of the family, private property and the state', in *Selected Works of Marx and Engels*, one volume edn (London: Lawrence & Wishart, 1968), pp. 449–583.

Engels, F. (1890), 'Letter to Schmidt', in *Selected Works of Marx and Engels*, one volume edn (London: Lawrence & Wishart, 1968), pp. 684–9.

Engels, F. (1895), 'Introduction' to the 'Class struggles in France, 1848–50', in *Selected Works of Marx and Engels*, Vol. 1 (Moscow: Progress Publishers, 1969), pp. 186–204.

Fine, B., Harris, L., Mayo, M., Weir, A., and Wilson, E. (1984), *Class Politics: an Answer to its Critics* (London: Leftover Pamphlets).

Gerstenberger, H. (1976), 'Theory of the state: special features of the discussion in the FRG', in *German Political Studies*, Vol. 2, ed. K. Von Beyme, M. Kaase, E. Krippendorf, V. Rittberger and K. L. Shell (London: Sage), pp. 69–92.

Gordon, P. (1984), 'Community policing: towards the local police state?', *Critical Social Policy*, Issue 10, Summer, pp. 39–58.

Gough, I. (1972), 'Productive and unproductive labour in Marx', *New Left Review*, 76, pp. 47–72.

Gramsci, A. (1971), *Selections from the Prison Notebooks*, ed. Q. Hoare and G. Nowell Smith (London: Lawrence & Wishart).

Gramsci, A. (1977), *Selections from the Political Writings 1910–20*, ed. Q. Hoare (London: Lawrence & Wishart).

Gramsci, A. (1978), *Selections from the Political Writings 1921–26*, ed. Q. Hoare (London: Lawrence & Wishart).

Griffiths, D. (1982), 'Housing: Labour's tangle over tenure', *New Socialist*, May/June, pp. 50–2.

Griffiths, D. (1984), 'A housing stance for Labour', in *Right to a Home*, Labour Housing Group (Nottingham: Spokesman), pp. 20–35.

Griffiths, D., and Holmes, C. (1984), 'To buy or not to buy . . . is that the question?' *Marxism Today*, May, pp. 8—13.

Hadden, T. (1972), *Company Law and Capitalism* (London: Weidenfeld & Nicolson).

Hall, S. (1977), 'The political and the economic in Marx's theory of class', in *Class and Class Structure*, ed. A. Hunt (London: Lawrence & Wishart), pp. 15—60.

Hall, S. (1979), 'The great moving right show', *Marxism Today*, January, pp. 14—20.

Hall, S. (1980), 'Popular-democratic *vs* authoritarian populism: two ways of "taking democracy seriously"', in *Marxism and Democracy*, ed. A. Hunt (London: Lawrence & Wishart), pp. 157—85.

Hall, S. (1984), 'The crisis of Labourism', in *The Future of the Left*, ed. J. Curran (Cambridge: Polity Press), pp. 23—38.

Hindess, B. (1981), 'Parliamentary democracy and socialist politics', in *The Popular and the Political*, ed. M. Prior (London: Routledge & Kegan Paul), pp. 29—44.

Hindess, B., and Hirst, P. (1977), *Mode of Production and Social Formation* (London: Macmillan).

Hirsch, J. (1978), 'The state apparatus and social reproduction', in *State and Capital*, ed. J. Holloway and S. Picciotto (London: Arnold), pp. 57—107.

Hirst, P. (1977), 'Economic classes and politics', in *Class and Class Structure*, ed. A. Hunt (London: Lawrence & Wishart), pp. 125—54.

Hirst, P. (1979), *On Law and Ideology* (London: Macmillan).

Hobsbawm, E. (1982), 'The state of the left in Europe', *Marxism Today*, October, pp. 8—15.

Hodges, D. C. (1961), 'The intermediate classes in Marxian theory', *Social Research*, Vol. 28, no. 1, Spring, pp. 23—36.

Holloway, J. (1979), 'The state and everyday struggle', mimeo, pp. 1—33.

Holloway, J., and Picciotto, S. (1976), 'A note on the theory of the state', *Bulletin of the Conference of Socialist Economists*, Vol. 3, no. 5, pp. 1—8.

Holloway, J., and Picciotto, S. (1977), 'Capital, crisis and the state', *Capital and Class*, 2, pp. 76—101.

Holloway, J., and Picciotto, S. (1978), 'Towards a materialist theory of the state', in *State and Capital*, ed. J. Holloway and S. Picciotto (London: Arnold), pp. 1—31.

Hunt, A. (1977), 'Theory and politics in the identification of the working class', in *Class and Class Structure*, ed. A. Hunt (London: Lawrence & Wishart), pp. 81—111.

Hunt, B. C. (1936), *The Development of the Business Corporation in England, 1800—1867* (Cambridge: Harvard University Press).

Hyman, R. (1984), 'Wooing the working class', in *The Future of the Left*, ed. J. Curran (Cambridge: Polity Press), pp. 90—9.

Jefferson, T., and Grimshaw, R. (1982), 'Law, democracy and justice: the question of police accountability', in *Policing the Riots*, ed. D. Cowell, T. Jones and J. Young (London: Junction Books), pp. 85—109.

Jessop, B. (1977), 'Recent theories of the capitalist state', *Cambridge Journal of Economics*, Vol. 1, pp. 353—73.

Jessop, B. (1982), *The Capitalist State* (Oxford: Martin Robertson).

Johnston, L. (1981), *Classes and the 'Specificity of Politics' in Marxism and Sociology* (University of Liverpool: unpublished Ph.D thesis).

Jones, P. (1980), 'Socialist politics and the conditions of democratic rule: notes on Marxism and strategies of democratisation', in *Marxism and Democracy*, ed. A. Hunt (London: Lawrence & Wishart), pp. 139—55.

Laclau, E. (1980a), 'Populist rupture and discourse', *Screen Education*, no. 34, pp. 87—93.

Laclau, E. (1980b), 'Togliatti and Politics', *Politics and Power*, 2, pp. 251—8.

Laclau, E., and Mouffe, C. (1981), 'Socialist strategy: where next?', *Marxism Today*, January, pp. 17—22.

Lea, J., and Young, J. (1984), *What is to Be Done About Law and Order?* (Harmondsworth: Penguin).

Lenin, V. I. (1902), *What is to be done?* (Peking: Foreign Language Press, 1973).

Lenin, V. I. (1916), *Imperialism, the Highest Stage of Capitalism* (Peking: Foreign Language Press, 1970).

Lenin, V. I. (1917a), 'One of the fundamental questions of the revolution', in *Collected Works*, Vol. 25 (Moscow: Progress Publishers, 1964), pp. 366—73.

Lenin, V. I. (1917b), *The State and Revolution* (Peking: Foreign Language Press, 1970).

Lenin, V. I. (1919), 'A great beginning', in *Collected Works*, Vol. 29 (Moscow: Progress Publishers, 1965), pp. 409—34.

Lenin, V. I. (1920), *Left Wing Communism, an Infantile Disorder* (Moscow: Progress Publishers, 1970).

Loney, M. (1983), *Community Against Government. The British Community Development Project, 1968—78* (London: Heinemann).

Lukacs, G. (1971), *History and Class Consciousness* (London: Merlin Press).

McDonnell, K., and Robins, K. (1980), 'Marxist cultural theory: the Althusserian smokescreen', in *One Dimensional Marxism*, by S. Clarke, V. J. Seidler, K. McDonnell, K. Robins, and T. Lovell (London: Allison & Busby), pp. 157—231.

McLennan, G. (1984), 'Class Conundrum', *Marxism Today*, May, pp. 29—32.

Marx, K. (1844), 'Economic and philosophical manuscripts', in *Early Writings* (Harmondsworth: Penguin, 1975), pp. 279—400.

Marx, K. (1847), *The Poverty of Philosophy* (Moscow: Foreign Language Publishing House, n.d.).

Marx, K. (1850), 'The class struggles in France, 1848—50', in *Selected Works of Marx and Engels*, Vol. 1 (Moscow: Progress Publishers, 1969), pp. 205—99.

Marx, K. (1852a), 'The eighteenth brumaire of Louis Bonaparte', in *Selected Works of Marx and Engels*, Vol. 1 (Moscow: Progress Publishers, 1969), pp. 394—487.

Marx, K. (1852b), 'Letter to Weydemeyer', in *Selected Works of Marx and Engels*, Vol. 1 (Moscow: Progress Publishers, 1969), p. 528.

Marx, K. (1857—8), *Grundrisse* (Harmondsworth: Penguin, 1973).

Marx, K. (1859), 'Preface' to 'A contribution to the critique of political economy', in *Selected Works of Marx and Engels*, Vol. 1 (Moscow: Progress Publishers, 1969), pp. 502—6.

Marx, K. (1862—3), *Theories of Surplus Value*, Vol. 1 (Moscow: Foreign Language Publishing House, n.d.).

Marx, K. (1863), *Capital*, Vol. 2 (London: Lawrence & Wishart, 1974).

Marx, K. (1863—6), 'Results of the immediate process of production', Appendix to *Capital*, Vol. 1 (Harmondsworth: Penguin, 1976), pp. 943—1084.

Marx, K. (1864), *Capital*, Vol. 3 (London: Lawrence & Wishart, 1974).

Marx, K. (1867), *Capital*, Vol. 1 (London: Allen & Unwin, 1938).

Marx, K. (1871), 'The civil war in France', in *Selected Works of Marx and Engels*, one volume edn. (London: Lawrence & Wishart, 1968), 248–309.

Marx, K., and Engels, F. (1846), 'The German ideology', in *Selected Works*, Vol. 1 (Moscow: Progress Publishers, 1969), pp. 16–80.

Marx, K., and Engels, F. (1848), 'Manifesto of the communist party', in *Selected Works*, Vol. 1 (Moscow: Progress Publishers, 1969), pp. 98–137.

Marx, K., and Engels, F. (1852), 'The elections in England – Tories and Whigs', in *Collected Works*, Vol. 2 (London: Lawrence & Wishart, 1979), pp. 327–32.

Meiksins Wood, E. (1983), 'Marxism without class struggle?', *Socialist Register*, pp. 239–71.

Meszaros, I. (1972), *Marx's Theory of Alienation* (London: Merlin Press).

Miliband, R. (1967), *The State in Capitalist Society* (London: Weidenfeld & Nicholson).

Miliband, R. (1973), 'Poulantzas and the capitalist state', *New Left Review*, 82, pp. 83–92.

Miliband, R. (1977), *Marxism and Politics* (Oxford: Oxford University Press).

Milne, S. (1984), 'It's the fall-out that matters', *Guardian*, (December).

Mouffe, C. (1979), 'Hegemony and ideology in Gramsci', in *Gramsci and Marxist Theory*, ed. C. Mouffe (London: Routledge & Kegan Paul), pp. 168–204.

Mouffe, C. (1981), 'Democracy and the new right', *Politics and Power*, 4, pp. 221–35.

Nicholls, W. J., and Carr, J. G. (1976), *Company Law and Practice* (London: Longman).

Nichols, T. (1969), *Ownership, Control and Ideology* (London: Allen & Unwin).

Nicolaus, M. (1967), 'Hegelian choreography and the capitalist dialectic: proletariat and middle class in Marx', *Studies on the Left*, 7, pp. 22–49.

O'Connor, M. (1985), 'Just what the country doesn't need', *Guardian*, (January).

Ollman, B. (1972), 'Towards class consciousness next time: Marx and the working class', *Politics and Society*, Vol. 3, no. 1, pp. 1–24.

Phillips, A. (1985), 'Class warfare', *New Socialist* (February), pp. 28–31.

Picciotto, S. (1979), 'Review of Sumner's "Reading Ideologies"', *Tribune* (September).

Pimlott, B. (1984), 'The politics of the popular front?' in *The Future of the Left*, ed. J. Curran (Cambridge: Polity Press), pp. 195–210.

Poulantzas, N. (1972), 'The problem of the capitalist state', in *Ideology in Social Science*, ed. R. Blackburn (London: Fontana), pp. 238–64.

Poulantzas, N. (1973a), 'On social classes', *New Left Review*, 78, pp. 27–54.

Poulantzas, N. (1973b), *Political Power and Social Classes* (London: New Left Books).

Poulantzas, N. (1975), *Classes in Contemporary Capitalism* (London: New Left Books).

Poulantzas, N. (1976), 'The capitalist state: a reply to Miliband and Laclau', *New Left Review*, 95, pp. 63–83.

Poulantzas, N. (1977), 'The new petty bourgeoisie', in *Class and Class Structure*, ed. A. Hunt (London: Lawrence & Wishart), pp. 113–24.

Poulantzas, N. (1978), *State, Power, Socialism*, (London: New Left Books).

Przeworski, A. (1977), 'Proletariat into class: the process of class formation from Karl Kautsky's "The Class Struggle" to recent controversies', *Politics and Society*, Vol. 7, no. 4, pp. 343−401.

Reiner, R. (1978), 'The police, class and politics', *Marxism Today*, March, pp. 69−80.

Riddell, P. (1983), *The Thatcher Government* (Oxford: Martin Robertson).

Rose, N. (1980), 'Socialism and social policy', *Politics and Power*, 2, pp. 111−35.

Rubin, I. I. (1972), *Essays on Marx's Theory of Value* (Detroit: Black and Red).

Savage, S. P. (1984), 'Political control or community liaison? Two strategies in the reform of police accountability', *Political Quarterly*, Vol. 55, no. 1, pp. 48−59.

Schuller, T., and Hyman, J. (1984), 'Forms of ownership and control: decision-making within a financial institution', *Sociology*, Vol. 18, no. 1, pp. 51−70.

Scott, J. (1979), *Corporations, Classes and Capitalism* (London: Hutchinson).

Showstack Sassoon, A. (1980), *Gramsci's Politics* (London: Croom Helm).

Smith, D. (1983), *Police and people in London: Vol. 3; A Survey of Police Officers* (London: Policy Studies Institute).

Thompson, G. (1982), 'The firm as a "dispersed" social agency', *Economy and Society*, Vol. 11, no. 3, pp. 233−50.

Togliatti, P. (1979), *On Gramsci and Other Writings* (London: Lawrence & Wishart).

Tomlinson, J. (1982), *The Unequal Struggle? British Socialism and the Capitalist Enterprise* (London: Methuen).

Urry, J. (1973), 'Towards a structural theory of the middle class' *Acta Sociologica*, Vol. 16, no. 3, pp. 175−87.

Urry, J. (1981), *The Anatomy of Capitalist Societies* (London: Macmillan).

Weir, A., and Wilson, E. (1984), 'The British women's movement', *New Left Review*, 148, pp. 74−103.

Westergaard, J., and Resler, H. (1975), *Class in a Capitalist Society* (London: Heinemann Educational Books).

Wright, E. O. (1978), *Class, Crisis and the State* (London: New Left Books).

Zeitlin, M. (1974), 'Corporate ownership and control: the large corporation and the capitalist class', *American Journal of Sociology*, Vol. 79, no. 5, pp. 1073−1119.

Index

reductionism 6, 7, 50, 54, 58, 61, 64, 72, 77, 85, 104–17, 121–4, 141
Reiner, R. 98–9
relative autonomy 6, 7, 50, 56–62, 63, 65–70, 73–4, 85, 98, 122
Riddell, P. 126
Risorgimento 159
Rose, N. 129
Rubin, I. I. 90

Savage, S. P. 136–7, 139
Schuller, T. and Hyman, J. 133
Scott, J. 19, 130
separation of ownership and control 13–15, 25, 30, 34–41, 132–3
shareholding 37–41
Showstack Sassoon, A. 60–1
smashing the state apparatus 54–6
Smith, A. 90
Smith, D. 137
social totality 8, *passim*
  polarisation of structure/action in constitution of 122–3
socialism
  Marx on the development of 30–3
  as working class politics 85–103
socialist civil society 61–2
socialist objectives 140, 141–2
socialist pluralism 8, 127, 140–5
Stalin, J. 3
state
  as bourgeois form 73–6
  civil society distinction 60–2, 78
  as class domination 50–6
  class-historical view of 71–6

derivation theory 65, 70–6
France 56–7
monopoly capitalism 65
non-unitary 134–40
power and class power 52, *passim*
and socialist political intervention 134–40
as strategic field 68–9
theory 49–81
Straw Bills 136

teleology 4, *passim*
tendency for the rate of profit to fall (TRPF) 73–4
Thatcherism 126–9
Thompson, G. 130, 132–3
Togliatti, P. 60
Tomlinson, J. 131–3, 142
trades unionism 101–3, 131
Trotskyist left 125

unproductive labour
  see productive/unproductive labour
Urry, J. 79, 86

war of manoeuvre 61
war of position 61
Weberian sociology 123
Weir, A. and Wilson, E. 125–6
Westergaard, J. and Resler, H. 19–22
women's movement 1, 125–6
Wright, E. O. 38, 43–4, 85, 91–6, 99

Zeitlin, M. 19